To Woody —

A good Friend —

Phil Jackson

FIFTY YEARS OF CHEERS AND JEERS

PHIL JACKSON

Published by
Rainmaker & Associates, Inc.
P. O. Box 3422
Gainesville, GA 30503

1st printing, 1997

Library of Congress Catalog Card Number 97-067277

ISBN 0-9655242-1-3

Sammy Smith, Editor
Cover design by Sandy Jackson and Hulsey Graphics

Printed by LifeSprings Resources, Franklin Springs, Georgia

ACKNOWLEDGEMENT

"Hardy went down to botanize in the swamp, while Meredith climbed towards the sun. Meredith became, at his best, a sort of daintily dressed Walt Whitman: Hardy became a sort of village atheist brooding and blaspheming over **the village idiot**."

The above bit of poetry, lifted from *The Victorian Age in Literature,* has absolutely nothing to do with the contents of this book.

TABLE OF CONTENTS

CHAPTER 1

THE LAUDABLE LATE FORTIES

World War II was over and we had won. Consequently the years of the late 1940's were fun and upbeat as the sports world returned to normal with quests for a couple of high school state championships, and some exciting doings in industrial league baseball.

Best meets best for state title

December 10, 1947

The flatlands of south Georgia will be trembling this weekend when the "Colossus of the North," Gainesville High, meets the "Terror of the South," Valdosta, for the state Class B football championship.

This game, to be played on neutral ground in Albany Friday night, will pit the best offensive team in the state, Valdosta, against the best defensive team in the state, Gainesville.

Valdosta's Wildcats have averaged more than 33 points per game and are heavy favorites over the Red Elephants of Gainesville.

However, Gainesville is undefeated through 12 games so far because the Elephants have given up only two touchdowns all season, one in a 6-6 tie with Griffin and one in a 46-6 win over Athens.

In the other 10 games, Gainesville's great defense blanked Winder, Elberton, Waycross, Decatur, Marietta, Russell, West Fulton, LaGrange, Spalding and Rockmart.

Gainesville's good defense will be tested by Valdosta's big and fast offense that features backs Billy Grant and Sonny Stephenson.

Gainesville's starting team will have Walter Byrd at quarterback, Jack Roberts and Frank Barrett at halfbacks, Marvin Free at fullback, Jimmy Henson and John Hulsey at ends, Leland Rew at center, George Newton and Ben Spears at guards, and George Dobbs and Curtis Pethel at tackles.

Among Gainesville's top defensive specialists are Tubby Strickland, Jim Pound, Arthur Ballew, Ernest Nivens and Billy Rogers.

This game will mark the first time a Gainesville High team has ever played for a state championship in the new era of playoffs.

Three Gainesville teams back in the 1920's were declared state champions under a ranking system.

Local observers say this Gainesville team, coached by Drane Watson, is the best since those 1920's teams that were coached by Joe Pittard.

Fast Cats sweep Phants

December 13, 1947

Valdosta's Wildcats got a clinching score in the final minutes Friday night to defeat Gainesville's Red Elephants 24-12 for the state Class B football championship in Albany.

Although Valdosta led most of the time, the game was still up for grabs until just a few plays before the end when the Wildcats clicked on a touchdown pass to clinch the contest.

The Wildcats were both big and fast as backs Sonny Stephenson and Billy Grant led an offense that featured effective end sweeps.

Gainesville's vaunted defense had to spend too much time on the field as the Gainesville offense could sustain few drives.

Halfback Jack Roberts, who came close to getting loose on broken field runs a number of times, was outstanding both ways for the Elephants.

Valdosta jumped out front to stay with a 48-yard drive in the first quarter as fullback Brooks scored from close in.

Running from a number of unusual formations, Valdosta drove again in the second quarter and moved 80 yards with Stephenson scoring from the one.

Gainesville got back in the game when Roberts hit Jimmy Henson with a long pass and fullback Marvin Free went around end from 10 yards out to score, and Valdosta led 12-6 at the half.

Gainesville pulled even in the third period when Roberts set up a score with a pass interception. Walter Byrd passed 16 yards to John Hulsey for the touchdown and a 12-12 tie.

But Valdosta came right back with end sweeps again, and Stephenson ended a drive by going off tackle for nine yards and an 18-12 lead.

Late in the fourth quarter, Valdosta got moving in the air and scored the clincher when Grant faked an end sweep and fired a scoring pass to end Metcalf.

Although Gainesville made a nice comeback to make a game of it, Valdosta was the dominant team most of the contest.

Pitching, gift win state title

June 5, 1949

Two superb pitching performances, with a gift win in between, led Gainesville's Red Elephants to the state Class B baseball championship in tournament play held at City Park here.

Coach Drane Watson's Elephants, who struggled through a somewhat erratic regular season, got it all together at just the right time to sweep tournament games from Albany, Canton and Fulton of Atlanta before crowds of some 1,200 fans each night.

The successful run began with Gainesville's Jack Roberts blanking Albany on one hit, 1-0.

3

In a dual between two of the best high school pitchers in Georgia, Roberts fanned 14 batters and gave up only one bloop hit as Albany's Phil Clark struck out 15 and allowed only five hits.

The lone run came in the sixth inning when Roberts singled to center and circled the bases when the ball got past the Albany centerfielder.

Centerfielder Marvin Free had two of Gainesville's hits.

In the Canton game, it appeared the Elephants were eliminated as Canton carried a 5-2 lead into the bottom of the ninth inning.

But Canton fell apart in the field, committed four errors in the inning and allowed Gainesville to score four runs.

Winning pitcher John Hulsey, who gave up only six hits, got Gainesville's only hit in the bottom of the ninth. The tying and winning runs scored when the Canton catcher threw wildly into left field with two out.

First baseman Roberts and third baseman Harold Griggs each had two of Gainesville's eight hits.

In the state championship game against Fulton, Gainesville fans were wanting Roberts to return to the hill to sew up the title.

But it was husky righthander Bobo Smith who strolled to the mound and came through big, hurling a five-hit shutout for a 9-0 Gainesville victory.

Smith helped himself at the plate with a two-run triple as Roberts went three-for-three.

Larry Pardue, Curtis George and Free also had big hits for the Elephants.

Defensively, the Elephants performed much better during the state tournament than at any other time during the season with Curt Moore at second, George at shortstop, Ferris Wing, Lewis Spain and Free in the outfield, Griggs at third, Larry Pardue catching, Hulsey pitching and playing first and Roberts pitching, playing first and the outfield.

Red Barron's place

July 13, 1975

This time of year, when football teams are preparing to open practice sessions, always conjures up memories of the days when many high school teams went up into the hills to pre-season camps.

The idea behind such camps was to isolate the players from the distractions of civilization, make sure they got plenty of sleep on cool mountain evenings, feed them lots of fresh vegetables in a dining hall, and devote almost all daylight hours to conditioning and learning how to play football.

4

Most of the time, however, players managed to find plenty of distractions; they sneaked out at night or played cards under blankets with flashlights, ate the food served and managed to steal even more, and invented all kinds of short cuts to ease the drudgery of practice sessions.

I remember 1947 when I was manager of the Gainesville High team and we journeyed up past Mountain City in Rabun County to a camp operated by Red Barron, who was a former Georgia Tech great and not the guy whom Snoopy chases on his Sopwith Camel.

To say the least, we enjoyed an eventful stay. The Marist team from Atlanta was also there and the two teams scrimmaged each other. The fights that followed some of the practices were always interesting.

Drane Watson was the coach at GHS then, and after the first couple of nights, he conducted a raid on the sleeping quarters and confiscated all the playing cards and dice. One guy managed to hide a single die, and it was used to keep a small-number, high dice game going.

There were also some repercussions when we were allowed to attend a square dance at Mountain City and some of the guys came in contact with some illicit liquid refreshment.

But the incident that sticks out most in my mind had to do with a cross-country run. The team was to run along a dirt road, pass over a small mountain and finish up at the practice field.

As manager, I was to make the trek equipped with a snake-bite kit in case someone encountered an angry reptile.

There was also a prize for the top finishers. Being of slight build, such a run was not too much of a problem for me. There was very little excess on my 5-5, 105-pound body. So, I decided to try for one of the top spots.

I struck out fast and soon was at the front of the group. I made it through the wilderness of the mountain and had it going smoothly when I got back on the road. Finally, sweating and gasping for breath, I made it back to the practice field and flopped proudly to the ground near Coach Watson who stood waiting.

But I soon sensed he wasn't too pleased with my performance. Hands on his hips, his legs widespread and his neck veins standing out, he screamed: 'Jackson! You idiot! What are you doing back here in front of everyone?"

I could not understand his chagrin. I thought I had put forth a valiant effort, especially since I was only the manager. In a stream of loud words, Coach Watson informed me that I was carrying the snake-bite kit, and was supposed to trail the pack so that I would be available to administer first aid. That thought hadn't crossed my high school mind. But Coach Watson's words firmly implanted the idea that I was supposed to maintain some sense of duty and responsibility.

You learn things in odd ways.

That football camp apparently paid off, however, because the Gainesville High team of that year went some 12 games without a defeat and didn't lose until meeting Valdosta in the state finals.

I don't know whether the success was because of the dice games, the fights, the moonshine or the cross-country run.

Actually, I think it was Coach Watson's neck veins.

Industrial baseball diverse, popular

July 1, 1997

In 1948, possibly the most popular sport in the Northeast Georgia area was industrial league baseball.

The league, closely followed by loyal fans for years, featured aging players, some of them former pros, and young guys right out of high school.

In July of 1948, the first annual Georgia-Carolina Industrial League All-Star Game was played at Gainesville's City Park baseball diamond.

That year the league was made up of local mill teams from New Holland, Gainesville Mill and Chicopee, along with teams from Jefferson Mills, Commerce, Clarkesville Trade School and Oconee, S.C.

The game was between league-leading New Holland and an all-star team selected from other league teams.

Two of the all-star players, one a former major leaguer and the other a future major leaguer, were examples of the diversity of the league.

The captain of the all-star team was Jefferson's Alf Anderson, a Gainesville native who had starred at the University of Georgia, with the minor league Atlanta Crackers and had made it to the major leagues with the Pittsburgh Pirates before and after World War II.

Also on the Jefferson team was 18-year-old Jim Umbricht who had just graduated from Decatur High School and would go on to play with the Pirates and Houston in the National League from 1959 until 1963.

There were some other former minor league pros involved in the 1948 all-star contest.

Dean Evans, manager of Gainesville Mill and the all-star team, had some good years in the old Georgia-Florida and South Atlanta leagues.

Guy Miller, a Commerce infielder, had played in the Pacific Coast League and Louis Hallman of Clarkesville had toiled in the South Atlanta League.

Over the years, many pros passed through the industrial leagues.

6

New Holland had one of its many excellent teams in 1948 and had five players named to the all-star roster. They were second baseman Fuzzy Wood, pitcher-outfielder Jake Miller, catcher Charlie Lay, third baseman Pete Morgan and centerfielder Nolan Riley.

The remainder of the New Holland host team had Ralph Chapman at shortstop, Robert Marchbanks pitching, Bige Hollifield at first base and Dub Jones in the outfield.

The all-stars had Anderson at shortstop, Hallford at second, Miller at third, Blanton Griffin of Chicopee, Erskine Grogan of Oconee and Jim Sosebee of Clarkesville in the outfield, Clyde West of Chicopee at first, Lloyd Black of Clarkesville catching, and George McCollum of Commerce pitching.

Another all-star pitcher was Chicopee's Doc Harper who was fresh out of Lyman Hall High School. Willard Wood of Chicopee was also a member of the all-stars along with Lefty Buchanan of Oconee and catcher Lyons of Commerce.

Some 1,500 fans, one of the largest crowds ever for baseball at City Park, watched the all-star game that was won by the all-stars, 7-6, when Anderson doubled across two runs in the top of the ninth inning.

Umbricht came on to preserve the win when he set New Holland down in order in the bottom of the ninth.

Roberts fabulous in the forties

July 11, 1997

The Gainesville area sports scene in the late 1940's was epitomized by the exploits of Jack Roberts, believed by many to be the greatest high school athlete in Georgia history.

In the four-year period from 1946–49, Roberts literally did everything in every sport for the Gainesville High School Red Elephants, and even more.

It would be impossible to break down each and every athletic deed ever done by Roberts who was a wiry, 150-pounder with more natural ability than any local athlete before or since.

Roberts was an All-State selection in football, baseball, basketball *and* track.

In football he was a great broken-field runner and pass receiver who also passed, kicked and played defense.

In baseball he could, and sometimes did, play any position, but was truly a great pitcher.

In basketball, he averaged scoring in double figures when teams seldom scored more than 40 points.

He probably could have performed any event in track, but he specialized in the high jump and broad jump. He was state high jump champion in 1949.

One of Roberts' most versatile performances took place during the Ninth District playoffs held in Athens.

In the morning, Roberts pitched and won a nine inning baseball game. That afternoon he took part in track and won the high jump, the broad jump and ran anchor man on the winning relay team.

In baseball, Roberts pitched a few no-hitters and a blazing fastball led to high strikeout totals.

In a state tournament baseball game in 1948, Roberts hooked up with Thomaston's Hugh Frank Radcliff who was rated by many as the greatest high school pitcher in the state.

Roberts fanned 20 batters in that game and Radcliff struck out 24. Both teams had some fielding problems and Gainesville won the game, 7-6.

Roberts also excelled in sports not on the high school agenda.

The first time he ever touched a golf club, he shot in the 80's.

In 1948, he was city swimming and diving champion.

And you didn't want to mess with him on a pool table. He was a nine-ball and snooker expert.

When Jack graduated from Gainesville High, he was offered a major league baseball bonus to sign with the Brooklyn Dodgers.

However, he chose to go the University of Georgia to play football and baseball.

He earned a first-string halfback spot on the Bulldog football team and became the ace pitcher on the baseball team.

In 1952, Roberts set a Bulldog record by striking out 103 batters in 112 innings. He pitched Georgia to the SEC championship and into the District 3 NCAA finals.

After college, Roberts had to fulfill a military obligation and this dimmed what had been a bright future in baseball.

But it didn't stop him, for he not only went on to coach on both the high school and college level; he also fashioned some impressive pro pitching credentials.

He was in the St. Louis Cardinals' chain and posted a 42-27 professional record. His best year was in 1956 when he was 14-3 with Allentown, Pa. of the Class A Eastern League and Rochester of the Class AAA International League.

In 1953 Roberts pitched in the South Atlantic League and went against a young player for Jacksonville named Henry Aaron.

Said Roberts at the time, "If Henry Aaron keeps going like he is now, he will be a big star in the major leagues one of these days."

So, you see, Jack Roberts was not only a great athlete, he knew talent when he saw it.

CHAPTER 2

THOSE BURNING BRIGHT YEARS OF THE TIGERS

Before the public schools were integrated, black athletes played their own games among themselves and met with great, if often unrecognized, success.

Birth of the Tigers

August 31, 1950

Twenty-three youngsters are working out daily on the Fair Street High School athletic field in an attempt to gain positions on the black community's first football team.

Principal C. W. Daniels said the grid hopefuls have been taking part in "shaping up" exercises under the direction of Coach Belton James.

James, who teaches shop and mathematics at the school, has some football experience and will handle the team.

Charles C. Myers, who is connected with the Hall County Vocational School, is assisting James.

Members of the community Progressive Club first got the idea for a football team at Fair Street to keep more boys in school and curb juvenile delinquency.

The club sponsored a concert featuring musician Graham Jackson and raised more than $700 in gate receipts and contributions as a result of the concert held at the Gainesville Civic Building.

Some money is still needed to buy 22 uniforms to dress out two full teams. Some equipment has already been ordered, and the rest will be sent for when the money is raised.

Daniels said possibly three games would be scheduled this season, and the first one would probably be held the latter part of September.

Tigers win Georgia title

December 9, 1956

Gainesville's Fair Street Tigers won the state football championship Friday night by overcoming an outclassed heard of Evans County Longhorns, 27-0, on a muddy City Park gridiron.

It was evident in the first quarter that the Tigers had the Class B title safely tucked away as the green and white clad boys from Claxton were clearly no match for the hustling, talented Tigers of Coach E. L. Cabbell.

The running of Gene Carrithers, Clifford Stephens and Ellis Cantrell—coupled with timely passing by Cecil Young and great receiving by Arthur Moss—stunned the visitors from South Georgia early and never let them into the ballgame.

Fair Street took the opening kickoff and quickly marched 66 yards to a touchdown. The running of Carrithers sparked the drive. The speedy halfback dashed 22 yards to put the ball on the Claxton five and one play later, Cantrell banged over from three for the score. David Camp booted the point for a 7-0 lead and the Longhorns were through for the evening.

The Tigers got another quick tally when Camp recovered a fumble on the Evans County 28. Quarterback Young lofted a soft pass which Moss leaped up and caught with one hand to put the ball on the Claxton nine. Young ran two straight quarterback sneaks for the touchdown. Carrithers grabbed a bad snap from center on the conversion and circled right end for the extra point and a 14-0 lead.

The ensuing kickoff saw the Tigers get one of the strangest touchdowns of the year. Camp's boot bounced to the Longhorn end zone where a Claxton back fumbled it twice, kicked the ball and then—for some unknown reason—decided to let it lie in his end zone. But Fair Street's Thomas Carter and Camp gleefully fell on the ball for the TD. The point was missed and the score stood 20-0 at halftime.

Carrithers picked up the final touchdown on the most beautiful run of the night. He took an early third quarter punt on his own 22-yard line, deliberately weeded his way through tacklers for some 15 yards, suddenly broke into the clear and sped 78 yards for the score. Cantrell cracked over for the EP and the count rose to 27-0.

A penalty on Stephens' 33-yard touchdown dash and a fumble on Claxton's six-yard line killed two other Fair Street chances.

It was the first state title in the history of Fair Street football, and the championship game climaxed a 12-1 season for the spectacular Tigers.

Fair Street grabs 2nd state title

December 22, 1957

Fair Street's Tigers—sparked by the explosive clutch running of tiny Gene Carrithers—scored early and late here Friday night to defeat a fine Thomasville team, 13-7 and gather in their second consecutive Georgia football championship.

With only three minutes and 40 seconds left on the City Park clock and the score knotted at 7-7, Carrithers cracked over tackle on a crossbuck, bounced off one tackler and fought his way six yards for the winning touchdown.

Tiger end Arthur Moss intercepted a pass to stop the last Thomasville threat with 30 seconds remaining. Fair Street ran out the clock and jubilant players lifted Coach E. L. Cabbell and Carrithers to their shoulders for a victorious ride across the gridiron.

Thomasville's Douglas High Lions were a tough, spirited eleven that featured the keeper runs and passes of quarterback Charlie Ward and the quickie dashes of halfback Roosevelt Reed, but hulking Clarence Niles, David Camp, Johnny Keith, and William Johnson furnished the defensive knocks for Fair Street when they were needed.

Fair Street jumped off to a quick lead in the first quarter. Fullback Ellis Cantrell set up the score when he returned to punt 20 yards to the Thomasville 19.

On the first play, quarterback Cecil Young lofted a high, floating spiral to Moss who gathered it in over his shoulder in the Lion end zone. Cantrell plunged over for the point and a 7-0 lead.

Thomasville's offense suddenly came alive midway in the second quarter and the Lions drove 69 yards for the tying tally. Ward's keeper cutbacks off tackle were the main thrusts of the push. Reed bucked over from the two. Ward carried for the extra point and the teams went out for the half.

Fair Street's strutting band presented an imaginative Christmas show during intermission that was complete even to a formation of a tree with blinking, colored lights.

Neither team could muster an effective offense in the third quarter and through half of the final period.

But just when it seemed a tie was in the books, the Tigers started their winning drive from their 41-yard line with six minutes remaining.

Carrithers got it underway when he burst through center, cut to the sidelines and sped 32 yards to the Thomasville 27. Cantrell hit for five, Carrithers for six, Clifford Stephens for five and Cantrell for five again to the six.

Little Gene then fired his 135-pound frame through for the big one and Fair Street had its 16th straight victory and the state Class A trophy.

Cabbell was the man

October 2, 1994

The many athletic accomplishments by Gainesville's black high schools during the days of segregation were directed by Coach E. L. Cabbell.

Cabbell first coached at Fair Street High and then E. E. Butler High and tutored many successful sports teams.

He also coached at Gainesville Junior High and with the Gainesville Parks and Recreation Department.

Cabbell coached locally from 1951 until 1970, almost two decades, and was a regular winner.

His top accomplishments came in 1956 and 1957 when his Fair Street football teams won two straight state championships. He also coached the Fair Street girls basketball team to a state title.

In 1962 at Butler High, Coach Cabbell lived up to a reputation for making his teams stronger as seasons went along.

In the opening football game of the season in 1962, Butler lost to the Lemon Street Hornets of Marietta in a rout, 39-6.

Later in the season, the Tigers won the Region 2-A championship by beating the Hornets 19-18 behind the play of Larry Castleberry, Jesse Butts and Melvin Tanner.

Spurred to improvement by that early loss, Cabbell's Tigers ended that season with a 5-1 record in the sub-region.

Fair Street set local records

June 21, 1997

Gainesville's Fair Street Tigers set a couple of modern local records over a three-season span while they were racking up black high school state football championships.

From November of 1956 until November of 1958, the Tigers went 24 consecutive football games without a loss and picked up state championships in 1956 and 1957.

Fair Street had 21 straight football victories when McDonough held the Tigers to a 0-0 tie in October of 1958.

The Tigers stretched the unbeaten string to 24 straight with a 13-7 win over Griffin in November of 1958.

The streak came to an end when Greensboro took a 7-0 win over the Tigers one week after the Griffin win.

It was ironic that Greensboro had been the last team to beat Fair Street in November of 1956 before the unbeaten string started.

Fair Street's unbeaten streak record is considered a modern mark.

The all-time local record was set back in the 1920's by Gainesville High School before the days of championship playoffs.

Those Gainesville teams, under Coach Joe Pittard, from the end of the 1922 season into the 1926 season won 35 straight games.

In the days of big Dude

June 21, 1997

If a true sports legend still lurks in the memories of those around in the days of segregation in Gainesville, it would have to be Clarence (Dude) Mack.

A tall, rangy guy blessed with all sorts of athletic ability, Dude could play any game ever invented with much skill. But he was best known as a pitcher for the Gainesville Eagles, one of the many black "town teams" in small communities across the South in those days.

The Eagles played most of their games at their own Midway Park located just off Athens Highway, and they also played quite often at the baseball field then located at City Park.

The Eagles played against other traveling teams from the North Georgia area and from Atlanta where many such teams were based.

Dude made his name as a pitcher during the 1949 season when he beat just about everybody in sight and won 34 games. An old-fashioned high, hard fastball was his best weapon, and posting more than 10 strikeouts a game was the norm for Mack.

One of the best and more entertaining teams of the day were the Atlanta Clowns.

Dude got a typical win over the Clowns on a Sunday afternoon at Midway Park in 1950.

Dude struck out 11 batters and gave up just two hits as the Eagles took a 9-2 victory. James Randolph homered for Gainesville and Billy Clyde had a pair of hits.

There was plenty of showtime during the game.

One of Dude's favorite acts was to call all his fielders in to sit in a circle around the mound.

While his teammates clapped and swayed in unison to his pitching motion, Dude would proceed to strike out the side on nine pitches.

There were those skeptics who said the act required voluntary cooperation from the opposition.

Mack's nickname was placed permanently on a young white high school athlete of the day.

Young and strong Billy Joe Thompson played for Gainesville High School at the time.

Dude once hit a long, long home run to deep right field at City Park.

In a high school game soon afterward, Thompson hit a homer into the same area.

At that moment, Billy Joe, who would go on to star in football for the Georgia Bulldogs, became known as Dude Thompson.

CHAPTER 3

LOCAL FOLKS MAKE GOOD

Athletes from the Gainesville area did much on a state level, and many advanced on to higher accomplishments, not only in sports, but other endeavors as well.

Tech signs GHS duo

December 7, 1959

One of football's hottest courtships came to a blissful climax in the wee hours of Monday morning when Georgia Tech signed Gainesville's Billy Lothridge and Billy Martin to gridiron grants-in-aid.

The signing came as no real surprise since rumors were heavy all season long that the two stars were inclined to lean toward Tech as first choice. But as the recruiting wars waxed hotter, a host of educational institutions were seeking the services of the Red Elephant captains.

According to recruiting rules, the gates officially opened for signings at midnight last night. It was soon after that the 175-pound quarterback and the 215-pound end made their choice to wear the white and gold.

It was probably a relief for the lads to settle the issue. Maybe now they will be able to eat a quiet meal without finding recruiters in the mashed potatoes.

Georgia Tech broke a drought of its own by acquiring the Gainesvillians. It has been more than a decade since a Gainesville High footballer went to the Flats via the scholarship route. The last one was Billy Brice, a guard off the 1948 team. The last Red Elephant to see any regular action for Tech was Ben Spears, a guard who performed as a specialist on the Jackets' kicking teams during the two-platoon days of the early 1950's.

Since that time, Gainesville has been regarded as a Georgia Bulldog stronghold with most of the prospects being channeled to the state university.

As one Tech assistant coach put it: "For a long time we considered sending missionaries into Gainesville to prepare the way for recruiting. There are so many Georgia folks there, the Bulldog barks outnumber the chicken clucks."

Mr. Cool and the Jolly Giant

October 25, 1961

Gainesville's Billy Lothridge and Billy Martin are among the very few players ever to come off the same high school team and make it so big and so quick with a major college power.

As sophomores at Georgia Tech, these two former Red Elephant stars are already holding down key positions for a team which is rated the seventh best in the country.

Lothridge, a 184-pound quarterback, leads Tech in scoring with 25 points, does all the kicking and is second on the team in total offense with 228

18

yards gained. Martin, a 6-4, 226-pound end, starts on offense and is the Jackets' second ranking pass receiver with 97 yards gained. His big hands aren't his only weapon since he has blossomed into a fine blocker.

It seems only fitting that these two should remain together. They've been teammates since their grammar school days and have formed a great combination for years. In football, Lothridge throws and Martin catches; in baseball they serve as pitcher and catcher. Even in high school basketball one of their favorite plays had Lothridge faking an outside jump shot and snapping a pass to big Martin under the bucket.

HOMETOWN HEROES

Former Gainesville High School sports stars Billy Martin (left) and Billy Lothridge (right) talk with Gainesville businessman Ross Burnes during "Billy Day" ceremonies in 1963. The special day honored Martin and Lothridge who have just completed All-American college football careers at Georgia Tech.

As athletes, they appear to be entirely different types. Lothridge excels because he is a cool, determined and sometimes even grim performer. He thrives on competition and has always done a serious job of beating the other fellow.

On the other hand, Martin is a jolly giant. He has been known to break out in broad smiles during a game and he has always been a crowd favorite. It seems he plays well because to him sports still mean fun and games. To many, college football is drudgery, but Martin apparently enjoys it.

Both actually came through suddenly for the Jackets. As a freshman last season, Lothridge was going unnoticed in early practice sessions because he is not a flashy, spectacular athlete. But as one Tech coach put it: "We began to notice that when Lothridge was at quarterback, the team moved better. He has that intangible talent for leadership."

The coaching staff considered red-shirting Martin for a year. But as Coach Bobby Dodd revealed "Ol' Billy started snagging that ball and blocking like he really wanted to play. He's probably the most improved man on the squad."

Tech hit the jackpot when it won the recruiting battle for Mr. Cool and Jolly Giant.

The Paul that refreshes

August 8, 1965

It was just like one of those television commercials. The annual Georgia prep all-star football game had just ended. Outside the Grant Field dressing room door stood South Hall's Jerry Paul, alternately answering questions from admirers and taking breathless swigs from a king-size Coca-Cola.

Sweat poured from his blond head and face, turning his star-spangled jersey an even darker crimson. Uniformed guards kept the crowd from crossing into the roped off area of the dressing room ramp. But this didn't keep fans from reaching over to shake Paul's hand or pat him on the shoulder pads as he stood near the rope.

Paul was happy as a young man who had just played the key role in winning his state's biggest prep sports classic. He didn't say this or even hint at it. But everyone in the crowd at the rope and those pouring past toward the exits were well aware of it.

Just minutes earlier, Paul had entered the game as a substitute for injured Neal Lazenby of Sylvan. His North team trailed 2-0 in the final quarter and was showing no signs of doing very much about it. Paul did something about it immediately. In three big plays and less than four minutes, he converted a loss into a 14-2 victory.

The first time he touched the ball he sped and twisted on a punt return some 30 yards to the South 27 to set up a touchdown which Dykes' Billy Payne later scored on a short pass from Sylvan's Donnie Hampton.

Just seconds later, Paul breezed up from his defensive safety position and picked off a South pass to put the North in business again at the Rebels'

43. The next play, he drifted out from his flanker position, grabbed a short pass from Hampton and again showed his speed and elusiveness down the right sideline to the South 15. Hampton later ran for the touchdown from the three.

Because he threw for one score and got another, Hampton beat out Paul in the voting for most valuable back in the game. But Hampton would never have had the opportunity to be a hero had Paul not set things up.

"I didn't even think I was going to get to play," grinned Paul over the Coke bottle. "I pulled a muscle just after practice started and missed all the scrimmages. By the time I got back in shape, the starting lineup was set. If Lazenby hadn't gotten hurt (pause for swallow of Coke), I wouldn't have gotten a chance."

North Coach Bill Chappell of Dalton was very glad Paul got his chance. He almost wrenched Paul's arm off shaking his hand after the two touchdowns and then added a big hug at midfield just after the game ended.

When asked about the South team, Paul replied: "They were big but didn't move too well." Compared to Jerry, very few high school boys move well. He was state Class AA 100- and 200-yard dash champion two years in a row, added the broad jump title this year and was voted Class AA back of the year in Georgia for gaining more than 1,000 yards rushing at South Hall.

As Paul talked, smiled, swigged and took time to lean over the rope and give his mother a kiss on the cheek, a very smug-looking fellow stood in the background. It was Georgia Tech scout Spec Landrum, the man who bird-dogged Paul for two years and finally got his name on a Yellow Jacket grant-in-aid. Landrum nodded and waved to acquaintances in the crowd. He seemed to be saying "I told you so" to everyone there.

Paul's performance in the all-star game was a fitting climax to a brilliant prep career. He has always been a coach's dream as an athlete as well as an outstanding student. Polite, quiet, unassuming and unimpressed with his own accomplishments, he is a joy to see and know.

We can compare him only to Mary Poppins. Both are too good to be true and both can fly.

The exploits of Bucky

October 19, 1966

The small news item out of New Brunswick, N.J., reads: "Ernest (Bucky) Curtis of Vanderbilt is among 153 nominees in the 'After 1910' category for the National Football Hall of Fame."

In case you have forgotten, Bucky Curtis was the leading pass receiver in the nation when he made All-America at Vanderbilt in 1950 and was the first Gainesvillian to be so recognized.

The son of long-time Riverside Military Academy athletic director Col. Jack Curtis, Bucky played for RMA and followed the late Coach Red Sanders to Vanderbilt and a brilliant collegiate career.

Now an executive with a paper company in Cincinnati, Ohio, Bucky has been thrust back into the gridiron spotlight by his nomination for a coveted hall of fame berth.

A highly popular athlete and person during his young years here, Bucky played four years of varsity football (freshmen were eligible then) at Vandy from 1947 through 1950. A gangly but effective pass receiver at Riverside, Bucky blossomed into one of the most feared offensive weapons in the Southeastern Conference. Some of his exploits are worth recalling.

His biggest season was 1950 when he caught 27 passes for 791 yards and nine touchdowns. This led the nation, was an SEC record at the time and led the conference in scoring. He also set another SEC record by averaging 23.9 yards per catch. Incidentally, the fellow throwing to Bucky in those days was Bill Wade who just three years ago helped the Chicago Bears win a National Football League title.

For his play in '50, Bucky was named first team All-America on offense by *Look* magazine, the Football Writers Association of America, Bill Stern's selections and was named either second or third team by Associated Press, United Press International, Collier's and NEA. To show his versatility, he was named defensive All-America by International News Service.

Bucky's greatest individual game of the season came during a 27-22 victory over Alabama. Curtis caught six passes for 196 yards and two touchdowns. The first pass play, Wade-to-Curtis, came just three minutes after the game started and was good for 85 yards. Bucky took the ball at midfield and out-ran Bama's Butch Avinger to the goal line by 10 yards. His total for the day missed the existing national collegiate record by just seven yards.

That same season, Bucky figured in one of the most spectacular plays in the history of southern football. It came in the Florida game with less than two minutes to play and the Gators safely ahead, 31-20. Curtis started the play by clutching a 29-yard pass from Wade. As the covering Florida defensive back closed in for the tackle, Bucky lateralled to halfback Mac Robinson and blocked the Gator defender. Curtis kept his feet, followed Robinson downfield and when the latter was being tackled at the 22, took another lateral and crossed the goal standing up. The play covered 76 yards.

Ernest Jackson Curtis Jr. was a great and complete football player. Even more than that, he was recognized here and everywhere he went as a sportsman and gentleman.

"Tough" Preston has his day

February 16, 1966

Gainesville's Preston Ridlehuber was honored by his hometown here last night as an overflow crowd of more than 300 persons gathered at the Elks home to heap praise upon the broad shoulders of the flashy young quarterback.

Amidst proclamations from the Governor, mayors of two cities and the state legislature, probably the most significant announcement of the evening came from University of Georgia publicist Dan Magill who revealed that Ridlehuber had been named to the All-Time Bulldog football team. This places the blond speedster in the company of such greats as Charlie Trippi and Frank Sinkwich.

Georgia Coach Vince Dooley and former Gainesville High Coach Graham Hixon were the most generous with their praise of Ridlehuber as a football player, all-around athlete and leader.

"Exciting and a great competitor," said Hixon of the 190-pounder. "Not only was he a great runner, but he was the best defensive safety man I ever saw in high school football. I had all the confidence in the world in Preston when he was running the football team. He knew where the goal line was and how to cross it."

Without qualification, Dooley stated: "Preston Ridlehuber is physically the toughest football player I have ever been associated with." Dooley related how Ridlehuber played four games last season with a knee injury that would have sidelined most players. "He did a terrific job for us despite this handicap."

Dooley recalled that a former coach of his, now at Clemson, remarked how he didn't think Georgia could win with Ridlehuber at quarterback. "I want to remind that gentleman that Georgia has now beaten Clemson twice with Ridlehuber at quarterback."

Bound for the San Francisco Forty-Niners of the National Football League, Ridlehuber was hailed by the coaches for his great ability as a kick returner and clutch passer.

Georgia defensive back Joe Burson, Ridlehuber's roommate for the last two years, brought howls of laughter as he related some of his experiences with Preston on and off the football field.

Speaking seriously, Burson said: "Georgia didn't start winning football games until Joel Eaves, Vince Dooley and Preston Ridlehuber got there. I'm proud to have known and played football with Preston Ridlehuber, and I'm proud to be a part of his day. I know of no one who deserves it more."

George Smith, speaker of the Georgia House of Representatives, stopped by to congratulate Ridlehuber prior to the banquet. During the festiv-

23

ities, proclamations and resolutions were read by Gainesville Mayor John Cromartie and Hall County Representatives Bill Williams and Joe T. Wood.

Georgia backfield Coach John Donaldson narrated a film of Bulldog football highlights of 1965 and paid special attention to great plays turned in by Ridlehuber. "He has that beautiful running style you just can't coach," he said. "You have to be born with it."

Ridlehuber, who sat quietly next to his mother and father, Mr. and Mrs. Howard Ridlehuber, presented a short, humble talk at the close of the evening.

After being presented with a plaque by Abit Massey, chairman of the steering committee of the Gainesville-Hall County Georgia Club which sponsored the event, Ridlehuber said: "I guess I'm just one of the luckiest guys alive. I was filling out a questionnaire from the Forty-Niners the other night and one question asked what I considered my greatest experience in life. I hope it hasn't been mailed yet because all this tonight has to be the greatest thing that could happen to anybody."

Better than Johnny Mize

March 22, 1967

Every baseball fan has heard of Johnny Mize, the powerful fellow who cut a mighty home run swath through both the National and American Leagues for many years. But what about a guy right here in Gainesville who was considered a better prospect than Mize when both got their first professional chance at the same time?

Walt Cooper is in his 21st year as a member of the Gainesville Fire Department. The current generation of baseball followers never heard of him. But just ask any old-time observers of the game. They'll tell you that when the St. Louis Cardinals sent down for Cooper and Mize back in the 1930's, Cooper was the name they were most interested in.

Now 55 years of age and a dispatcher with the fire department, Cooper still has those powerful forearms which were the trademark of a strong hitter in his day. He seldom talks of his playing days unless pressed, but he remembers the glory time of the game when it was vastly popular in even the smallest Georgia towns.

When he first attracted the attention of pro scouts, Cooper was in his early twenties and playing in the outfield for Gainesville Mill in the old textile league. He was fast and hit with power.

Younger than Cooper, Mize was a tall, strong first baseman for Piedmont College in his hometown of Demorest.

24

Mize and Cooper were first spotted by Lee Crowe, free lance scout, veteran player and operator of a billiard hall and cafe on Main Street. He got the Cardinals interested in the pair.

How interested were the Cardinals? Mr. Branch Rickey himself drove down into these Northeast Georgia hills in his "Twin-Six Lincoln" and transported both Cooper and Mize to Greensboro, N.C., a Cardinal farm club in the Piedmont League. What Cooper remembers most about the luxurious auto was that it had a cigarette lighter which stretched on a long cord from the dashboard all the way into the back seat.

Cooper and Mize were not strangers, having played with and against each other on various occasions. Many times they were on local "all-star" teams which got together to play special July Fourth contests against such strong amateur aggregations as Buford, Dixisteel and Tubby Walton's Atlanta All-Stars.

It was midseason when Cooper and Mize reported to Greensboro, and they were immediately put through training paces.

The first hint of any dissatisfaction on Cooper's part came when the Cardinal instructor wanted to change him from an outfielder to a second or third baseman. Walt had never played anywhere but in the outfield or at first base.

During batting practice, pitchers were instructed to put all they had into their pitches to surprise prospect Cooper. Walt responded with a fine hitting show, sending a few out of the park. But the instructors wanted to change Cooper's batting style. He could never understand why.

After about two weeks, as Cooper puts it, he "just wasn't used to taking that kind of stuff" and he returned home. Young and brash, Cooper refused to undergo the discipline and forced training methods.

As for Mize, who was a more easy-going type than Cooper, he stuck it out and became one of the game's great stars. He led the National League in batting (.349) and homeruns (28) in 1939. He led the loop in homers with 43 in 1940, 51 in 1947 and 40 in 1948. In the early 1950's, he was picked up as a pinchhitter by the New York Yankees and helped them with a couple of world titles.

Cooper was satisfied to return to Gainesville Mill and play in local competition until he was past 30. Many fans can still remember some of the shots he hit into the lake back of right field at Gainesville Mill.

True, the training methods were foreign and unacceptable to the young Cooper. But many of his fans say he just got too far away from home where he "couldn't hear that mill whistle."

They also still say he was better than Johnny Mize.

The silent shatterer

September 19, 1967

If any athlete ever found himself a unique place to play college football it is Gainesville's Charlie Gignilliat.

You seldom will find any detailed newspaper write-ups about football at the University of the South of Sewanee, Tenn. But if you prefer that rare and quiet balance between athletics and academics, then Sewanee is the place.

Gignilliat, who was a one-man-gang performer for Gainesville High some four years ago, is a 190-pound senior tailback for Coach Shirley Majors at Sewanee.

Gignilliat probably could have earned a scholarship at a major college had he so desired. But he chose Sewanee where they take their football just seriously enough to play it well but not seriously enough to make any national headlines.

Gignilliat is a true triple-threat player who has been a standout passer, runner and kicker throughout his career at Sewanee. As a sophomore he led the College Athletic Conference in punting with a 42.0 average. There are plenty of guys in the major college and pro ranks who don't boot that well.

Gignilliat learned his football the hard way. When he inherited the first string quarterback job at Gainesville High, he succeeded Preston Ridlehuber and Billy Lothridge. No vaudeville performer ever had to follow a tougher act than that.

Besides having to endure comparisons with the greats who went before him, Gignilliat also was on a manpower-short GHS team which was forced to play in Class AAA. Despite all this, Gignilliat proved to be one of the toughest performers ever to play for the Red Elephants.

Not only did he take his lumps doing his triple-threat offensive duties but he also played safetyman on defense and led the team in tackles game after game. He was a devil-may-care defender who preferred this contact head-on and at full speed. The opposition at times took advantage of his eagerness, but none ever overcame his aggressiveness.

When he gradated from GHS, he had followed well in the very large footsteps of those who went before.

As a defender and punter, I firmly believe Gignilliat would have done well with any Southeastern Conference team. But apparently he didn't care for that life, so he now enters his fourth season playing against such schools as Milsaps, Randolph-Macon, Centre, Kenyon and Austin. His school has about 800 male students, is located on the quiet Cumberland Plateau and is owned by 21 southern dioceses of the Episcopal Church.

26

I think Charlie Gignilliat has done very well for himself and should have a banner season this year. But when I think back over some of those shattering tackles he made at GHS, I find it difficult to associate him with 21 southern dioceses of the Episcopal Church.

The Jolly Giant bows out

July 20, 1969

Because of the nature of the guy involved, I just can't force myself to write the usual "farewell" article concerning the retirement from pro football of Gainesville's Jolly Giant, Billy Martin.

Normally, such an event calls for a rather maudlin recount of athletic achievements topped off by a tearful pat on the back and a choked-up cry of "well done!"

If I did this, that big ox would laugh in my face.

Although I've known and followed the career of Martin since he was a gawky Little League baseball player some 17 years ago, few truly serious words have ever passed between us. Sports have always been fun and games for Billy, and all my conversations with him are filled with laughs.

Even the termination of a long and successful reign as a darn good football player isn't enough to make Martin wax serious.

When I called him at his Atlanta home last Tuesday to ask about future plans, he quickly remarked: "Alex Hawkins and me are gonna open up a barber shop. I'm gonna cut hair and he's gonna operate the back room."

In the past, some folks have been fooled by Martin's congenial, happy-go-lucky manner. When he and cohort Billy Lothridge were given football scholarships to Georgia Tech, there was talk that Martin might be too easy-going for the rigors of college football.

If you don't believe Martin has a hidden toughness, just ask Joe Namath. When Tech upset Alabama, 7-6, in that memorable 1962 game at Grant Field, Billy played a tremendous game at defensive end and literally rattled the expensive bones of quarterback Namath.

In fact, in a national magazine article that came later, even Alabama coach Bear Bryant remarked about "rough play" on the part of "that big number 88." This coming from the Bear is somewhat like John Dillinger calling Baby Face Nelson a crook.

There was also that time in 1959 when Martin, bearing an appendectomy scar only two weeks old, came off the bench to help Gainesville High beat Avondale, 13-12, in one of the biggest and best prep games ever played.

Later that same school year, Martin scored 22 points in a state finals basketball game while playing on an ankle so badly sprained and bloated it made you sick to look at it.

Sure, ol' Billy's a 6-4, 245-pound stack of laughs, but you don't make All-America at Georgia Tech and play five years of pro football with the Chicago Bears, Atlanta Falcons and Minnesota Vikings unless you have more going for you than a sense of humor.

Pro football is a rugged game, but Martin enjoyed one of his biggest laughs during the opening game of the past NFL season between Minnesota and the Falcons. Billy had been traded by Atlanta to the Vikings prior to the season and was playing tight end against his old team.

In the second quarter, Martin snared a 15-yard touchdown pass from quarterback Joe Kapp and this ignited the Vikings on to a 47-7 rout. I remember watching on television as Martin trundled off the field after the catch. He was clapping his hands and I swear I could hear that big guffaw of his.

Now an executive with a development corporation in Atlanta, Martin is a sartorial picture in suits and alligator shoes. I can't help but chuckle when I see this because I contrast it with the first time I ever saw him in a Little League game. They could not find a uniform big enough and it was hard to tell whether he was inside it trying to get out or outside trying to get in.

Still only 26 years old, Martin has decided to give up games for business. But his decision was made mainly so he would spend more time with his 17-month-old son Billy and wife Barbara.

So, with the strains of Auld Lang Syne being played by Spike Jones in the background, the Jolly Giant rides off into the sunset on his attaché case.

For Billy Martin and all of us who enjoyed watching him play, it was fun while it lasted.

Unforgettable Dude

July 23, 1971

The recent death of popular Billy Joe (Dude) Thompson stunned this community. If there ever was a fellow who perfectly fitted the "nice guy" mold, it was Dude.

An outstanding football player at Gainesville High, in the U.S. Navy and at the University of Georgia, Thompson had a host of fans. But, to me, his bright personality and his smiling outlook on almost everything overshadowed his athletic accomplishments.

His face was creased by an ever-present smile and laughter was his trademark. Adept as he was as a football player, he never took himself seriously as an athlete. To him, playing the game was a lark, even during the drudgery of the college game.

Dude was the key participant on two of the most memorable plays in Gainesville High's storied football history. Both took place during the 1951 season when Coach Clayton Deavers' Red Elephants won two championships.

On Oct. 12 of that year, the mighty Decatur Bulldogs rolled into town rated as a national prep power. Decatur had a winning streak of 29 straight games and was the talk of the state. But the victory string ended on City Park turf as big Dude and his mates pulled off a resounding 12-0 upset.

The clinching play in that win came in the third quarter with GHS nursing a shaky 6-0 lead. On an end around play, the 190-pound Thompson got outside, literally ran over Decatur's heralded Al Browning and stomped 69 yards for a touchdown.

Later that season, in a sub-region playoff game against Spalding High at Grady Stadium in Atlanta, Gainesville was faced with what appeared to be certain defeat. With only 10 seconds to play, the score tied at 12-12 and GHS trailing by penetration, the Elephants faced a fourth down and five situation at their own 35-yard line. The fans had already given up hope, but the Elephants apparently hadn't.

With the final second ticking away, quarterback Bud Cummings fired a pass that Thompson caught in Spalding territory carried all the way for the winning touchdown. Those on hand could hardly believe it had happened.

Dude entered the Navy after high school, played in the Hula Bowl and won all-service honors. After his discharge, he went to Georgia on a football scholarship and was a center and linebacker on the 1959 Southeastern Conference championship team and played in the 1960 Orange Bowl when the Bulldogs topped Missouri, 14-0.

When his playing days were over, Dude enjoyed nothing more than spinning humorous yarns about his career and he made himself the butt of most of the stories. And the way Dude could relate incidents, with that deep drawl of his, listeners were usually already in stitches before the tale ended.

One of his favorites concerned the 1959 Florida game when Georgia's Charley Britt intercepted a pass and ran it back 100 yards for a touchdown.

Thompson was in the game at linebacker when the play occurred. "I saw Britt intercept the ball at the goal line," Dude recalled. "So, I decided to turn on my blinding speed and lead a bunch of interference. I didn't mind when Britt passed me, and it wasn't too bad when that stumpy-legged little Florida guard went by. But when that fat, pot-bellied referee breezed by me, I decided to just let Britt score without my help."

It was always a pleasure just talking with Dude because he could brighten your day with a few words. Show me a guy who knew Dude well and didn't like him, and I will show you a guy in dire need of social therapy.

It was a pure joy knowing big Dude. It's a shame that death can't be more selective. It seems like 10 nice guys have died instead of just one.

A rare product

January 26, 1976

When the Gainesville Touchdown Club observed "Tommy West Day" here Saturday evening, it was actually honoring a real live product of the club's youth athletic programs.

No, I don't mean the TD Club manufactured, constructed or created Tommy West's physical being and athletic ability, but it did motivate him and provide a vehicle for his development as an accomplished player of games. This was culminated in the fact that West was given a free college education in exchange for his services as a football and baseball player.

West has just completed a fine four-year career as a scholarshipped athlete at the University of Tennessee. For three years he has been one of the best tight ends in Southeastern Conference football, and his bat has spoken with authority in SEC baseball competition. Consequently, Tommy doesn't owe anyone anything. He has paid all his debts through performance.

West came through all the levels of sports. He was outstanding in the TD Club's Little League baseball and midget football leagues. At Gainesville High, he was all-state in football and excellent in baseball and basketball. He was selected in the major league baseball draft by the Chicago Cubs, but chose to take a football scholarship to Tennessee. There is a possibility that pro football is in his future, maybe as a linebacker. If not, his athletic life is already more complete than most.

So, the TD Club, Saturday night at the Civic Center, thanked West for being a shining example of why the club exists as an organization dedicated to young people who need athletics as an outlet for their abundant energy, or just something to do to occupy their spare time.

There was nothing unique about the program. In turn, everyone who got up to speak sang the praises of West as an athlete and as a person. Being familiar with both aspects of West's life, I personally concur with all that was said. There was a proclamation from the mayor and the state legislature, along with the gift of a television set. Simply, it was a nice affair.

The point of all this is to emphasize the fact that Tommy West is somewhat of a rarity. More than 99 per cent of the kids who participate in athletic programs such as those supported by the Gainesville Touchdown Club, will never even come close to getting major college scholarships.

This is the best reason why junior athletic programs should have the support of a community. The programs should not be designed to develop super athletes. They should not be designed to overemphasize winning. They should not be designed to entertain adults. They should not be designed as baby-sitting services. They should be designed simply to provide healthy, enjoyable and useful activity for young people in the midst of their formative years.

Tommy West's emerging from such a program is a bonus. His role is that of an example, and he fills it well.

Harry could wing it
May 16, 1976

There is much talk these days of the times turned in by high school and college track men as they zip along in soft shoes on smooth surfaces so fast that timers need a quick thumb on the stopwatch to record the fleeting seconds.

But, the question arises, are modern sprinters so much faster than they were some 25 years ago when equipment and conditions were so very different? Yes, they probably are, but comparisons are interesting.

There is a fellow here in Gainesville named Harry Wing, who in 1952 was running times comparable to modern standards, and he was doing so wearing leather shoes with long steel spikes, on tracks constructed of rough cinders.

Now an optician who is concerned with healthy eyesight, Wing could really test your eyes with his speed in those days.

An outstanding football and baseball player at Gainesville High School, Wing did not even take up track until his senior year. All he did was set a state record of 10.1 seconds in winning the Class A 100-yard dash, he tacked on the 220 and also won both these events in the State All-Class meet, and did the same thing in the Southern Relays at Birmingham, Ala.

At the same time, out at Riverside Military Academy here, there was one Tony Luizzo who consistently ran the 100 in 9.8 seconds. Luizzo nipped Wing in the Georgia Junior AAU meet that year.

In the summer of '52, Wing played in both the North-South prep all-star football and baseball games, and his speed steadily improved. He and Luizzo both attended the University of Florida and teamed up with another fast guy there named J. "Papa" Hall.

As a freshman at Florida, Wing ran an official 9.6 and even had a 9.4 which was wind-aided.

Wing was on his way to becoming one of the South's truly fine all-around athletes. He was football starter at a defensive back position as a freshman at Florida. He was on the Florida team that almost upset mighty Georgia Tech which was on the way to a perfect 12-0 record and the Sugar Bowl.

But Tech averted defeat when some guy named Pepper Rodgers kicked a late field goal for a 17-14 win.

Wing's blossoming athletic career came to an end his sophomore season. In a game against Louisiana State, which was building toward a national championship under Paul Dietzel and his "Chinese Bandits," Wing suffered a severe knee injury which resulted in some paralysis of his leg. He was through, but his career was as dashing as it was brief.

Besides the injury, Wing still carries other physical mementos. There are traces of cinders under his skin as the result of falls, along with scars from being spiked in the legs by sprinters' shoes of the day.

More than likely, Harry Wing, and others of his era, could have equalled today's times had conditions been the same.

Yep, it's easier to run on today's tracks, vaulters use fiberglass sling-shots instead of bamboo poles and highjumpers land on foam rubber cushions instead of having to spit sawdust.

But those fans who saw Harry Wing run were just as thrilled and enter-tained as the spectators of today who have to look quick to see some guy run 100 yards in 9-nothing.

Big year for big Mike

August 1, 1976

If pre-season predictions hold true, the 1976 football season should be a biggie for tackle Mike Wilson of the University of Georgia who may well end up with more prizes than a gumball machine.

Wilson, a formidable figure at 6-5 and 255 pounds, is the strapping lad who went from Johnson High School here to almost instant stardom at Georgia. After a freshman season as the Bullpups' outstanding blocker, Mike became a starting defensive player on the varsity his sophomore year. But because a bevy of good running backs needed some operating room, Wilson went back to offense as a junior last season and was one of the big reasons the Bulldogs gained a record number of yards rushing.

Fondly nicknamed "Moonpie" by his teammates, Wilson was recognized as a second team All-Southeastern Conference selection in 1975, but he is being touted for much more than that in '76.

One pre-season football magazine has already picked him not only as an All-American, but as the outstanding lineman in the SEC. This is pretty heavy stuff for the unassuming Wilson who enjoys maintaining a "good ol' country boy" image.

Even though Wilson has already proven he is a premier player, how many honors he gathers will depend a great deal on how well the Bulldogs do as a team. Many outstanding individual players have been overlooked because they were associated with mediocrity.

But the Georgia team is getting some pretty good early recognition on its own. The Bulldogs have already been picked second to Alabama in the SEC and as high as 12th in the nation.

Normally, an offensive lineman operated in relative obscurity. But Wilson beat this rap last year when Georgia backs followed his blocking for gobs of yardage.

The folks in Wilson's home community will get to see him Friday from 2 to 4 p.m. when he appears at the College Square branch of Home Federal here.

You can't miss him. The only thing bigger than him on the premises will be the buildings.

Virtue named desire

December 12, 1976

If you think all those old sayings about sticking to a goal, hanging in there against all odds and never giving up are a lot of corny baloney, just talk to a young man named Bradley Roper.

Roper has just been given a full football scholarship to Georgia Tech after missing out on one two seasons ago, participating in another sport at another school in the interim, turning down a basketball scholarship, overcoming an injury, and just plain showing a heck of a lot of old-fashioned tenacity.

Roper was an outstanding all-around athlete in football, basketball and track at Johnson High School here. A solid defensive back in football, he wanted to play at Georgia Tech, so he went there on his own and went out for the team as a walk-on in 1974.

As luck would have it, he not only got lost in the crowd, he was caught up in the shuffle of a coaching change and the new NCAA 30-limit rule on scholarships. Besides that, Roper was beginning to fight a money shortage.

So, even though college football was still on his mind, he came home and went to Gainesville Junior College where he played basketball and participated in track for two seasons.

He was good enough in basketball at GJC to get a scholarship offer to LaGrange College. But he continued to suffer from the football bug, so he had a talk with Tech assistant coach Bill Curry.

"Curry is just a super guy," said Roper, "and when I told him I was thinking of trying football again, he said if that's what I really wanted to do, I should do it."

Last August, Roper reported to Georgia Tech football practice again, and again as a walk-on.

Adversity wouldn't stay away. He suffered a shoulder separation in drills and was out for six weeks. But he went back and worked out with the team the remainder of the season, fighting the battle of obscurity in the drudgery of practice sessions.

He got his reward a few days ago when the Yellow Jackets awarded him a full football scholarship at a free safety position. The scholarship goes into effect in January and he will have two seasons of playing eligibility.

Roper stands 6-2 and weighs 197 now, almost 30 pounds heavier than when he played basketball with the junior college here. Just how much action Roper will see at Tech is yet to be determined. But he is there on solid ground now.

Roper, always a friendly, polite guy, is making no big boast of his accomplishment. He states simply: "It was something I really wanted to do, so I just did it."

I believe there is a lesson for all of us in the saga of the determination of Bradley Roper.

He sells tickets, too

January 1, 1977

You've heard coaches say it a few hundred times: "This kid is just great. He does everyone for us but sell tickets."

Coaches over at Gainesville High School can go this one better, because all-around athlete Richard Brown actually sold tickets for the Red Elephants.

That's right. Brown, the leading ground gainer in the storied history of Gainesville High football, helped man the ticket table at GHS basketball games early on game evenings. He would then vacate that position to don a uniform and perform with the boys' team.

Friday afternoon, Brown, a 195-pound speedster, signed a football scholarship with Furman University. He might not sell any tickets at that school, but Furman is getting one of the most talented prep athletes ever to perform here.

Brown, a relatively quiet, calm young man who enjoys excellent rapport with his coaches and has no problems in the classroom, unobtrusively shattered almost every career ground gaining and scoring record on the football books at GHS.

Moving with a graceful, gliding gait that was a joy to watch, Brown gained 3,924 yards, scored 54 touchdowns and 326 points in three seasons as a starting running back for the Red Elephants. Every team he played on won championships either on the sub-region level or above.

As the starting tailback his sophomore and junior years, he gained more than 1,200 yards both seasons. He shifted to fullback as a senior and gained 1,049 yards. In those three seasons, he averaged gaining 7.56 yards each time he ran with the football.

His accomplishments didn't stop with football. He has been a starting forward on the basketball team the past two seasons. A good shooter and rebounder, Brown performed for teams that had a combined record of 47 wins and just seven losses plus two sub-region championship, one region title and a spot in this year's semi-finals of the State Class AA Tournament.

Oh, yes, Brown is also a sprinter on the track team.

One of those rare athletes who stepped right out of junior high school into a starting position, Brown will be sorely missed by the GHS coaching staff both as an athlete and person. Can you imagine the feelings of a coaching staff over the past three years knowing that a starting position in three sports was more than adequately filled by a young man who was totally dependable in competition, in the classroom, on extracurricular projects, and who even found time to hold down jobs during his sparse spare time?

Richard Brown is a unique young man. Furman is fortunate in getting him. Few schools sign athletes who can work, play, handle the books and even sell tickets.

The twilight single of Shanky Smith

May 21, 1978

When any athletic team enjoys a long string of success, you can usually go back to a single incident, one play, one hit, one catch or one throw that caused it all to happen.

In the case of Gainesville's Red Elephants, who have won eight straight playoff baseball games and are in the state championship finals next week, probably the key happening was a bouncing single off the bat of catcher Dexter (Shanky) Smith back on April 21.

Of course, almost every member of the Elephants, during the winning of 23 games and the losing of only three, has contributed greatly at one time or another with numerous clutch hits and plays. But that one little ol' single by Smith in the gathering twilight at the GHS diamond looms as the biggie.

On that day, GHS was playing Winder-Barrow in a regular season sub-region game. Winder had won an earlier meeting between the two, and the Elephants simply had to win to force a sub-region tie and stay alive. A Winder win would end the season for Gainesville.

The Elephants trailed by two runs going into the bottom of the sixth when big first baseman Ben Martin delivered a two-run single to tie the game. But Winder took a 4-3 lead in the top of the seventh.

In the bottom of the final inning, Smith came to bat with two out and the tieing run at second. With the entire season at stake, Shanky came through with that ground single back through the middle to knock in the run and force an extra inning. Billy Wilson won the game with a home run in the bottom of the eighth, but Smith's single made it possible.

Gainesville went on to beat Winder two straight games in the playoffs for the sub-region title, defeated Stephens County two straight for the region championship, knocked off Dalton twice in the first round of the state playoffs, and Thursday night sacked Avondale twice for the North Georgia championship.

Dexter O'Branty (Shanky) Smith is a 5-10, 160-pound senior who for the past two seasons has labored in the tough territory behind the plate for the Elephants.

Most catchers must endure a great deal of physical punishment, and Smith is rather small for the position. He has played most of this season on a bad leg, but has hung in there.

In the first game of the twin bill against Avondale, he was struck in the forearm by a pitch and suffered two burst blood vessels. But he got treatment between games and came right back and caught the second game, getting a

36

two-run single during Gainesville's six-run rally in the fourth inning that was the key to an 11-6 victory.

When the final out was made in the North Georgia championship sweep Thursday night, Shanky was one of the first to celebrate. He stripped himself of his catching gear in a matter of seconds and went leaping into the crowd of Gainesville players in the middle of the infield.

The Elephants might or might not go on and win the state championship. But they have their shot at it because Shanky got that hopping hit when it was needed the most.

State champs

June 1, 1978

Gainesville High's rather phenomenal streak of 10 consecutive playoff victories was fittingly climaxed yesterday when the Red Elephants won the state Class AA baseball championship and later received a standing ovation at Atlanta Stadium.

The Red Elephants beat the Marist War Eagles, 6-0, on a one-hitter by pitcher David Coker to sew up the Georgia championship at the Marist field in Atlanta yesterday afternoon.

By coincidence, it was Gainesville Night at the Braves-Reds game at Atlanta Stadium and the celebrating Gainesville team went as a group right from the playing field to the stadium.

When the Red Elephants filed into the stands along with Coach Jim Carter, the group was greeted by a standing ovation and the stadium message board flashed congratulations to the team.

Gainesville's playoff winning streak is probably some sort of record. Starting with the sub-region title series, the Elephants racked up 10 straight wins without a loss on the trek to the state championship.

They started by taking two straight from Winder-Barrow for the sub-region crown, swept two from Stephens County for the Region 8-AA title, opened the state playoffs by beating Dalton twice, took the North Georgia championship with a double header win over Avondale, and took the big trophy by beating defending state champion Marist 7-5 and 6-0.

Gainesville's 25-3 overall record sets school marks for victories and winning percentage.

It was the first baseball state championship for GHS in 29 years. The Elephants last won the title in 1949 and the coach of that team, Drane Watson, was in the stands to watch the current edition repeat the act.

"I couldn't be happier," said Watson after the game. "It was just wonderful. Coach Carter and his boys did a great job. I'm just as proud of them as if I were still coaching myself. I thoroughly enjoyed watching them play. It's a first class team from a first class school and town. It's just wonderful."

Everything fell into place for the team right on up to getting into the Braves game last night. It looked like the team was going to have to buy tickets to get in when a Union Oil Company official happened by, learned of the problem and gave the team 50 tickets he had available because it was also Union Oil Company Night at the stadium. He also later provided free hot dogs and Cokes for the team.

Coach Carter, an Athens native in his second year as GHS after shifting here from South Gwinnett High, also got a personal break in the wee hours of the morning.

After the Braves game, Carter went to Northside Hospital in DeKalb County to visit his wife Pat and their new baby daughter born on Tuesday. Carter left the hospital about 1:30 a.m. to drive home to Gainesville and gave out of gas on the 365 connector.

Stranded in the darkness of the early morning, Carter was given a lift by a General Motors employee on his way home from work. By the time Carter found an open service station and got gassed up again and into bed, it was after 5 a.m.

But like everything else, the sleep was good for Jim Carter. In fact, he slept like a champion.

Jody's big league debut a TV show

April 22, 1981

A small-town athlete making his debut in major league baseball usually has to call home or write a letter to tell his family about the experience. But not Hall County's Jody Davis, who made his first National League start with the Chicago Cubs against the St. Louis Cardinals yesterday.

Thanks to cable television, Davis' folks got to watch him play through the auspices of Chicago's WGN-TV which beams games here on Gainesville Cable Channel 9.

Davis, the former North Hall High School and Gainesville American Legion star, after five seasons in the minors, made it to the big time with the Cubs this season, but did not enter a game until yesterday. He was the Cubs' starting catcher and went the distance, although a number of Chicago pitchers didn't.

You could not call it a Frank Meriwell story, because the Cubs lost, 8-0, and Jody was hitless at the plate. But the tall, rangy redhead played his position well and drew praise from Lou Boudreau, former great major league manager and player who helps announce the Cubs' games.

Members of Davis' family here were not aware beforehand he was to play, but they all got the word.

Jody's mother, Mrs. Margie Davis, a rural mail carrier out of the Oakwood Post Office, was at her Oakwood home where she makes it a point to watch all the Cubs games. She said she was "thrilled" to get to see her son in his first big league game, but she kept getting interrupted by friends calling her to make sure she knew about the event.

Cecil W. Davis, Jody's father and superintendent of Hall County schools, was at his doctor's office, but got a call from his office about the game and managed to see some of the action.

Jerry Davis, Gainesville High School head basketball coach who coached his younger brother Jody at North Hall, was at home and got the word about the telecast from a friend, Bill Butler, longtime high school baseball umpire here. Jerry also got to view some of the contest.

Young Jody, the first local product to make the big leagues in modern history, was not at all shy about his cuts in the first at bat and hit a sharp grounder that Cardinal pitcher Andy Rincon stopped with a leaping stab to save a hit up the middle.

Davis was called out on strikes on a close outside pitch the second time up, and flied out to left in his final try.

He played well behind the plate, tagging out runner Ken Oberkfell trying to score from third and none of the Cardinals tested his throwing arm.

Jody did not hold back when there was a disputed call on a Cardinal hit off the left field wall. He joined right in with Manager Joe Amalfitano in discussing things with the umpires.

Right now, Davis is playing behind more experienced catchers Tim Blackwell and Barry Foote. Even though this might be considered a prejudiced view, Jody appears to be a better athlete than either. Also, Davis is a power hitter and might be a factor when he gets to play in the Cubs' rather small Wrigley Field.

Either way, Davis has made it to the big leagues, and those who care for him most enjoyed the unforgettable experience of viewing his first shot in the big time.

See Chester run

August 11, 1981

It was nice to see Chester Willis running again, even if it was for the Oakland Raiders and just for a brief stint against the Atlanta Falcons in last Saturday night's NFL preseason contest.

When Willis was at Johnson High School here some four years ago, he was enjoyable to watch with a football or as a sprinter in track. He was a blur and was once clocked at 9.6 seconds in the 100-yard dash.

He's a bit bigger now and has lost some of that dash speed during four seasons of taking football knocks at Auburn University.

Despite the fact that Chester was injured most of his senior season at Auburn, he was drafted by the Raiders in the 11th round and was still with them as of Saturday. Not being a high draft choice means the odds are against him, but the word is he has impressed the Oakland coaching staff.

He made a fine return of a kickoff against the Falcons and had a couple of other nice runs from scrimmage. It would be nice to see Chester stick with the Raiders because that might be a sign his luck is changing.

You see, during his career at Auburn, he had to play in the shadow of a couple of guys named Joe Cribbs and James Brooks. Cribbs made it immediately as a rookie with the Buffalo Bills last year, and Brooks is already making noise as a rookie with the San Diego Chargers this season.

Chester had to pull a lot of backup duty at Auburn during his first three seasons, and last year, with the departure of Cribbs, it was thought he would be used more alongside Brooks. But a knee injury held him back even though he was impressive when he did play.

In his senior football season at Johnson, he had some fine outings but his team didn't win a single game.

In track, he blazed by everybody in these parts and went to the state meet. You guessed it, he finished second in the state finals to a kid from Glynn Academy named Mel Lattany, now one of the premier sprinters in the world.

So, you see, timing has never been on Chester's side. He always has had to go against the best or near-best.

Even now he's trying to become a running back on a team that is the Super Bowl defending champion and has a crowd of experienced runners.

It may sound like a slogan from a hamburger commercial, but Chester Willis deserves a break.

Our first man in the Super Bowl

January 19, 1982

When offensive tackle Mike Wilson of the Cincinnati Bengals goes down into his first three-point stance under the canopy of the Silverdome at Pontiac, Mich., Sunday, it will mark the first time a local high school football product has ever played in a Super Bowl.

Wilson, who prepped at Johnson High here, went on to make All-America at Georgia and then took a stint in the Canadian League before settling down with the Bengals, will be a very visible figure against the San Francisco 49ers because he is one of the key pass protection blockers for Cincinnati quarterback Ken Anderson.

Wilson plays one of those positions where you are usually recognized only if you fail. Nobody notices and the TV announcers say nothing when you keep your man off the quarterback. But if he gets sacked, the world is told who missed the block.

One of the strongest men in pro football, "Moonpie," as he was known in his Georgia days, plays somewhat in the shadow of the more-publicized Anthony Munoz, the Bengals' left tackle. But Mike has probably done his job just as well. If he hadn't, Anderson wouldn't be the leading quarterback in the NFL.

The only other local high schooler who had a brush with a Super Bowl was Billy Lothridge, an All-America quarterback at Gainesville High and Georgia Tech, who almost made it to football's biggest show back in 1972.

Lothridge spent eight years in the pros, most of them with bad Atlanta Falcon teams. He led the NFL in punting twice, played some defensive back and even a bit of quarterback as a backup to Don Meredith with the Dallas Cowboys, the first team to draft Lothridge back in 1963.

Lothridge retired from the pros after the 1971 season. But late in 1972, Coach Don Shula of the Miami Dolphins called Lothridge into emergency service because Miami punter Larry Seiple was injured. Billy finished out the season as Miami's punter. But when the playoffs started, Seiple returned to the lineup and Lothridge was listed on the "taxi squad."

It was the year Miami posted that incredible 17-0 record and won it all. Lothridge did not get into the Super Bowl, but he was awarded a ring as a member of the team.

Actually, Lothridge's career was coming to an end at just about the time Wilson's was really beginning. It was within a few days of each incident in December of 1972 that Shula called Lothridge out of retirement and the University of Georgia decided to give a football scholarship to a big Johnson High tackle named Mike Wilson.

41

A couple of years ago, after Forrest Gregg was announced as the new coach of the Bengals, I remember talking with Mike right after he had come off the racquetball court where he keeps in shape during the off-season.

I asked him what he thought about Gregg as his new coach. "I understand he really works you awfully hard," Mike smiled. "Maybe that's exactly what we need."

Apparently it was, Mike.

Hardman hefts a heavy load

October 28, 1982

The mere fact he can push up more iron than most anyone else in this world does not tell the whole story of Gainesville's Tom Hardman.

Not only has Hardman endured the rigors of training, discipline and plain hard work required to become a world class powerlifter, while doing so, he has carried the additional load of medical school and serving his internship.

Last weekend Hardman broke away from his routine as an intern, journeyed down to the Atlanta Civic Center, entered the AAU-sanctioned Georgia Elite Powerlifting Championships and promptly set another world record in the bench press.

Hardman, who went into the meet as the world record holder at 609.5 pounds, did not settle for breaking his own world mark just once, he did it twice.

First he pressed 612.2 pounds. Then he came back later in the competition and put up 614.4 pounds to establish his current world best in his weight division.

At 6-3, 275 pounds and 29 years of age, Hardman said before the competition he had a simple goal: "I want to set a world record as an intern as I was able to do during each of my four years as a medical student."

Actually, Hardman understates his accomplishment. During the four years he was working to graduate from the Medical College of Georgia, he set nine world records in the bench press.

Also, Hardman is now being recognized as something more than just a muscleman who can lie on his back and pump iron. He has been selected as an Outstanding Young Man of America in recognition of "outstanding professional achievement, superior leadership ability and exceptional service to the community."

He was also recently chosen to serve on the Medical Committee of the United States Powerlifting Federation.

Most accomplished powerlifters are guys who work full-time at something related to the competition. They are either associated with a health spa or a gym, or are weightlifting instructors or coaches whose day-to-day routine keeps them somewhat close to the weights.

But Hardman's medical pursuits are about as far away from powerlifting as one can get. You don't learn much about heavy iron while handling surgical instruments.

Hardman himself takes a rather light-hearted look at what he has gone through when he says:

"As an intern, I've psyched myself into believing sleep is not essential. But at 275 pounds, eating is."

Former Red Elephants on ESPN

June 20, 1988

A former Gainesvillian, who's now a New York sports television producer, inadvertently found himself caught in a hometown nostalgia warp last week.

Warner Fusselle, who spent his young years in Gainesville when his father was pastor of the First Baptist Church here, is producer and narrator of the nationally-syndicated show "Major League Baseball Magazine."

Tonight, on ESPN at 7:30, the show will feature a cover story piece on Gainesville's Cris Carpenter, rookie pitcher for the St. Louis Cardinals.

Speaking by phone from New York the other night, Fusselle said, "The fact that both Cris and I have Gainesville backgrounds in the beginning had nothing to do with choosing him for the show."

"We wanted to do a feature on a young major leaguer from a small town," he said. "You know, the old 'hometown hero makes good' sort of thing. It just happened to turn out that Cris was the most perfect subject for such a piece. The Gainesville connection was just a coincidence."

However, when Fusselle got involved in gathering background, film clips, quotes, etc. for the show, he quickly found out how strong his youthful ties to Gainesville remain.

Himself a former baseball and basketball player at Gainesville High School, Fusselle first contacted an old teammate and friend, Gainesville attorney Cleon Nalley.

Nalley put Fusselle in touch with local background sources here such as Dr. Wendell Carpenter, Cris' father, and Jerry Davis, who coached Carpenter on two straight state championship basketball teams at GHS.

43

"When I heard the name Jerry Davis, it really struck a memory chord," said Fusselle. "I knew a guy with that name had been a good high school athlete at one of the county schools, but I couldn't remember which one."

"When I talked to Jerry," Fusselle said, "I realized he was once a catcher for old South Hall High School and I had played against him. Other memories of my Gainesville days really began to flood back them."

Fusselle had to do a lot of hustling around to gather material for tonight's segment on Carpenter, whose bright sports career began when he was National Hoop Shoot champion at age 9. He went on to stardom in three sports in high school, a punter for the Georgia Bulldogs, a pitcher for Georgia in the College World Series, Pan-Am Games competition and now the major leagues.

"On the major league level," said Fusselle, "We have clips of Cris' first major league pitch against the Braves, his first win against the Cubs—right on up to the other night when Cris lost to the Mets and was tagged for two home runs by Darryl Strawberry. We got it all."

One portion of the show is an interview with Carpenter. Look closely in the background and you will see some props that belong to Fusselle.

One is a Gainesville High letterman's jacket that Fusselle has kept through the years. And there are two small red elephant statuettes also visible.

Said Fusselle: "Would you believe I bought these two red elephants when I was on a trip to Venice, Italy? I couldn't believe finding red elephants in Italy."

Two other Red Elephants on tonight's show are Carpenter and Fusselle.

Playboy raises ire of former Elephant
September 6, 1987

A former Gainesvillian finds himself unavoidably embroiled in a situation that I'm quite sure he finds uncomfortable.

Dr. W. Douglas Skelton, who has held some of the highest medical administrative positions in Georgia and elsewhere, is now the provost and dean at Mercer University's medical school in Macon.

Because of his job, he finds himself engaged in a distasteful dispute with *Playboy Magazine,* one of the favorite targets of do-gooders and moralists.

However, in Dr. Skelton's case, he did not adopt the role as do-gooder or moralist, and he did not seek out *Playboy* as part of any part of any type of voluntary crusade.

The magazine chose his school, thus involving Skelton.

It seems *Playboy* recruited Mercer coeds to pose for photographs, nude and otherwise, and then advertised and promoted the picture spread as having taken place on the campus and in a dormitory at Mercer, a Baptist institution.

Actually, the pictures were taken at sites away from the campus. This incurred the ire of Dr. Skelton who is simply trying to protect the image of his school.

Skelton accused the magazine of "deceit and distortion" in its advertising methods because the interviews and shooting all took place in a Macon hotel room and in no way involved Mercer University.

Having to engage in such a dispute must grate on Dr. Skelton.

Back in the mid-1950's, Doug Skelton was a football lineman and an outstanding pitcher on the Gainesville High School baseball team.

He went on to graduate from Emory University School of Medicine, then progressed to:

• Psychiatric residency at Columbia Presbyterian Medical Center in New York.
• Two years with the U. S. Public Health Service as staff psychiatrist at the Federal Reformatory in El Reno, Okla.
• Director of Health Services at R. F. Kennedy Youth Center in Morgantown, W. Va.
• Faculty member in the Department of Psychiatry at Emory University.
• Began first drug abuse treatment program at Grady Hospital in Atlanta.
• Deputy superintendent of the Georgia Mental Health Institute in Atlanta.
• Director of the Division of Mental Health and Mental Retardation of the Georgia Department of Human Resources.
• Supervised a private psychiatric hospital in Smyrna.
  Named commissioner of the Georgia Department of Human Resources to oversee 29,000 employees and more than 100 health programs.
• Returned to a teaching position at Emory.
• Took his present position as dean and provost of Mercer's medical school in 1985.

Now, after all this impressive background, Dr. Skelton finds himself having to engage in a dispute with a girlie magazine.

While having to endure this situation, I'm quite sure Doug has probably wished, at least a few times, he was back pitching baseballs for the Red Elephants.

Certainly it was more fun, less complicated, and human behavior was more predictable.

But at least he hasn't lost his sense of sportsmanship.

He has announced, because of the circumstances, there will be no recriminations against the 11 coeds who took part in *Playboy's* promotional scheme.

Cris and Jody have their own Gainesville Day

May 22, 1988

They seldom hold a Gainesville Day at revered old Wrigley Field in Chicago. But they did last Thursday.

It wasn't a planned event.

It just happened in the course of a major league baseball game between the St. Louis Cardinals and the Chicago Cubs.

On the mound for the Cardinals was Gainesville's Cris Carpenter, a young rookie pitcher making only his second major league start.

Behind the plate for the Cubs was Gainesville's Jody Davis, a veteran and two-time National League all-star catcher.

In the end, Carpenter was the overall winner as he gave up only four hits and went the distance in the Cardinals' 5-1 victory.

It seemed fitting, however, that the Cubs' lone run came in the sixth inning when Davis drilled a Carpenter pitch deep off the ivy-covered wall in the left field corner for a double.

But that was the only noise for the Cubs as Carpenter was in complete control the rest of the way.

It was heady stuff for local fans who watched the game on WGN Chicago's TV superstation.

Cubs' announcer Steve Stone made an interesting point when he said something like, "Gainesville, Ga., is not a sprawling city. I wonder what the odds are against such a situation?"

They're high, Steve. Very high.

It's not the first time such a thing has happened, but it's rare.

Certainly one of the most interested television viewers was Coach Jerry Davis of Gainesville High School, who coached both his younger brother Jody and Carpenter during their formative athletic careers.

Jerry, while at North Hall High School, coached Jody, who was an outstanding prep basketball player.

When Jerry moved to Gainesville High, he coached two straight state championship teams, one with a perfect 30-0 record, that featured the sparkling play of Carpenter at guard.

Jerry was not "torn" between his two former stars as he watched Thursday.

"I just wanted them both to do well," said Jerry. "It crossed my mind that it might come down to a scoreless game in the ninth and Jody might hit a home run. That way, both would have played outstanding games.

"But I was very happy the way things turned out. I was pulling for Cris all the way because I want him to make it big up there."

Jerry pointed out that despite the difference in their ages, Cris is 23 and Jody 31, the two are good friends.

"They had supper together in Chicago a couple of nights before they had to face each other," said Jerry.

"Back before Cris signed with the Cardinals, he and Jody had a number of conversations about what might be ahead for Cris, and I think Jody probably had a few words of advice because of his experience."

Jerry feels that following major league baseball is now going to be twice as interesting with both Jody and Cris on the scene.

As announcer Stone pointed out, few towns the size of Gainesville can boast a pair of homegrown athletes on the major league scene at the same time.

Preston, meet Heidi

November 20, 1988

Just the other day, they observed the anniversary of one of the most memorable pro football games ever played.

Last Friday was the 20th anniversary of the infamous "Heidi" game that taught the television networks an important lesson: never leave a close TV game until it's over.

That game was between the Oakland Raiders and the New York Jets, and one of the key figures in the contest was a Gainesville athlete named Preston Ridlehuber.

What happened? The Jets were leading the Raiders, 32-29, with just over a minute remaining in the game.

That's when NBC-TV chose to leave the game to show "Heidi," a children's classic movie about a little girl cavorting in the mountains with some goats.

Much to NBC's chagrin—and the outrage of television viewers—the Raiders scored two quick touchdowns to pull out a 43-32 win.

One of those late touchdowns was scored by Ridlehuber, a Raiders'

47

specialty-team member, when he scooped up a fumbled kickoff and stepped into the end zone.

Ridlehuber was one of those talkative, reckless, free-spirit players who had a reputation for making things happen on a football field.

He had been an All-State and All-Southern quarterback at Gainesville High School.

A blond bundle of nervous energy, Ridlehuber for years held kickoff-return records at the University of Georgia, where he also was MVP in the 1964 Sun Bowl and gained national recognition in the Bulldogs' upset of Rose Bowl champion Michigan in 1965.

He was first drafted by the San Francisco 49ers, then played for the Atlanta Falcons before moving on to the Raiders.

While with the Raiders, he played under Coach Johnny Rauch, who also had coached Ridlehuber at Georgia.

No one was more perturbed about the "Heidi" thing than Ridlehuber.

Always somewhat of a hotdog athlete, Ridlehuber telephoned home after that game to check on the reaction of his parents and friends.

He couldn't believe it when he found out the game was taken off the tube before his scoring play.

Although Ridlehuber is best known by many as one of the "Heidi" figures, I remember him for an accomplishment that came later in his career when he made what is probably the biggest "league jump" in the history of football.

Released by the Raiders in 1969, Ridlehuber returned home to Gainesville.

It appeared his football career was over, except for the fact he was playing touch football here in a church recreation league.

Meanwhile, Coach Rauch moved from the Raiders to the Buffalo Bills, and one of the first things Rauch did was summon Ridlehuber to the Bills.

Now, most football buffs will claim that Johnny Unitas made a huge jump when he was picked out of a semipro league to become a great quarterback with the Baltimore Colts.

However, even though Ridlehuber's career ended due to a severe knee injury while he was with the Bills, his jump had to be the longest.

He is probably the only player ever to leap all the way from church-league touch football directly to the National Football League.

Ol' Preston always did have a flair for the spectacular.

Gainesville players vital for UGA

June 28, 1990

They're holding special ceremonies at the Gainesville American Legion baseball game here tonight to honor Jeff Cooper, who helped lead the University of Georgia Bulldogs to the national collegiate baseball championship this season.

Cooper, a product of East Hall High School and the Gainesville Post 7 Legion programs, was team captain and a key performer for the Bulldogs, who, rather surprisingly and impressively, won the NCAA College World Series recently.

Yet another local boy who made good, Cooper will be recognized tonight at Ivey-Watson Field when Gainesville meets Dahlonega in a Legion game.

Taking local baseball history into account, Cooper's presence on the Georgia championship team has to be considered either a coincidence, or a definite sign Georgia baseball recruiters might heed in the future.

You see, in the baseball history of the Bulldogs, they have reached the NCAA playoffs only three times, and each time a Gainesville area athlete was a key figure.

Cooper, of course, is the latest representative of our local community as he played on championship teams at East Hall and the Gainesville Legion before carrying his winning habit to Georgia.

In 1987, the Bulldogs got all the way to the College World Series for the first time and a big contributor to that team was Cris Carpenter, who was an all-sports standout at Gainesville High School and also a former member of the Gainesville Legion team.

And you really have to reach back in history to find the first time the Bulldogs made it to the NCAA regional playoffs.

It was in 1953, and one of the big reasons Georgia won the SEC title, and advanced to the regionals, was a hot-shot pitcher named Jack Roberts. Roberts was one of the great high school athletes of all time at Gainesville High before going to Georgia to play football and baseball, as did Carpenter some 30 years later.

In Roberts' day, college baseball teams played only about 30 games, as opposed to 60 or 70 scheduled games today.

Despite the comparatively shorter schedule, Roberts set SEC strikeout records that stood for more than 25 years.

And now Cooper, a solid all-around athlete and student, has carried on the infrequent tradition of Gainesville area baseball players contributing to Georgia's infrequent overall baseball success.

As I said, this might be just an infrequent coincidence.

On the other hand, Georgia baseball recruiters in the future might want to take a closer look at young baseball prospects developed in this area.

I can assure you that Cooper, Carpenter and Roberts are not the only good baseball players to come out of the Gainesville area.

There have been many others who went elsewhere and did well.

Let me add my congratulations to young Cooper for his accomplishments.

As the old-time baseball elders used to reluctantly say to youngsters displaying impressive skills, "You done good, boy."

Female football pioneer

August 15, 1992

News stories are coming out of Atlanta about a female placekicker on the Lakeside High School football team.

But it's not really news because that was made seven years ago by Shelly Garner of Gainesville High School.

When Camille Blackmore, a 160-pounder, kicked a successful extra point for Lakeside last season, it made her the second female ever to do so in a varsity game in Georgia.

In 1985, Gainesville's Garner became the first when she kicked an extra point in a 21-7 victory over Madison County.

"I'm glad to hear that someone else is kicking. You only live once, and I think you should try for anything you're interested in," said Garner, now an outreach coordinator for Girls Inc. of Northeast Georgia.

Although Garner was the first female to rack up points on the scoreboard, she wasn't the first to play on a high school team.

Earlier in the 1985 season, Shelia Gaffney of now-defunct Toombs Central in southeast Georgia became the first female to play in a varsity game in the state. The 140-pound senior fullback played in the second half of a 50-0 loss to Lyons, Toombs' 29th straight defeat.

Unlike most other females who have tried football, Garner lacked any extra size.

She was a petite blonde who stood 5 feet, 6 inches and weighed just 105 pounds.

West rise no surprise

December 1, 1993

Few folks in these parts were surprised when former Gainesville High star athlete Tommy West was named new head football coach at Clemson University recently.

Not that it was obvious that West would someday get the post at Clemson, but it was generally believed that West would be top dog at some top football school some day.

You see, West has been paying his athletic dues ever since he was an outstanding football, baseball and basketball player at Gainesville High in the early 1970's.

He went on to Tennessee where he was a star in both football and baseball.

After Tennessee, he had options in both pro football and pro baseball, but he chose coaching.

He paid his dues through the system as a high school coach, a college assistant at Clemson, Tennessee and South Carolina and last year was head football coach at the University of Tennessee-Chattanooga.

When Clemson called him back for the top spot, he was ready.

In fact, West was more than ready for Clemson because he had fallen in love with the school and football program when he was an aide to Head Coach Danny Ford there from 1982–89.

"Clemson just always felt like home to me," said West. "I feel like I've come back home."

West first attracted sports attention when he starred in Little League baseball and midget football in Gainesville back in the 1960's.

Even at that early date, lots of folks said Tommy West was destined to reach high places in the world of athletics.

Day of the rare twin titles

May 15, 1994

It's highly unusual for athletes from the same high school to win two state championships in one day at different sites.

But that is exactly what Gainesville High School sports products did almost simultaneously on the same Saturday evening in March of 1994.

The first part of this scarce scenario took place when the Gainesville High girls' basketball team capped off a fantastic perfect season by winning the Class AA state championship at Macon Coliseum.

51

Coach Manson Hill's lady Red Elephants, led by the play of star Mahogany Hudson, accomplished their feat by defeating Crim High of Atlanta, 36-35, in the state championship game.

It was the 30th consecutive victory for a Gainesville team that had lost the state championship game the previous season.

The young lady Elephants were still celebrating their big victory when, just a couple of hours later and a few miles northward, the second part of the state championship double dip took place.

It was in the Class AAAA boys' Georgia championship game played at Alexander Memorial Coliseum on the Georgia Tech campus in Atlanta.

It was there that Coach Doug Lipscomb, a former star basketball and baseball player at Gainesville High, directed his Wheeler High School Wildcats against Valdosta in the Class AAAA state decider.

Lipscomb had gone to Wheeler after serving as a teacher and assistant coach at Gainesville High.

In his very first season as head coach at Wheeler, he took a team that had a losing record the year before all the way to the state championship finals.

And he completed Gainesville's sweep of two state crowns by directing his Wheeler team to a 62-57 win over Valdosta for the state trophy.

According to newspaper quotes, after the Gainesville girls won, some of them said, "It's a dream come true."

After Lipscomb won his title, he said, "It's a dream come true."

Both dreams actually started at the same high school in Gainesville.

They were right about Damon

March 8, 1995

Just about everyone knew there was something special about Damon Evans soon after he and his family moved to Gainesville in the mid-1980's.

Football coach Bobby Gruhn knew when he recalled, "Damon came to us as a sophomore and immediately strengthened our football program."

Damon went on to set all-time Gainesville High pass receiving records in 1986–87.

Damon's teachers knew when they said things like, "He is a good student, and a great role model and has flawless character."

Evans was a member of Coach Vince Dooley's last recruiting class at the University of Georgia and played under Dooley and then Coach Ray Goff.

52

Said Goff, "Damon is the model of what every coach would like to have in his players and what every employer would like to have in his employees. A great work ethic, self-motivation and loyalty."

At Georgia, Evans attained a bachelor's degree in finance in four years and immediately enrolled in graduate school to pursue and complete a master's degree in sports management.

He took an opportunity to intern in the Southeastern Conference office where he concentrated his efforts on NCAA compliance issues for member schools.

At age 25, Evans was named director of compliance at the University of Missouri. He became one of the youngest executives in the nation to hold a front-office job in college sports.

"My philosophy is simple," said Evans. "It is to do the right thing. You can do what is right and still win."

Evans readily admitted that his goal is to someday become a collegiate athletic director.

Everyone always said there was something special about Damon Evans.

Lothridge last of a kind

February 27, 1996

When Gainesville native Billy Lothridge died recently, a rare breed of athlete died with him.

Lothridge, one of the greatest all-around athletes ever to play for Gainesville High School, died unexpectedly of a heart attack at age 54 at his Florida home.

Lothridge starred in football, baseball and basketball at Gainesville High in the late 1950's as he quarterbacked some championship football teams under Coach Graham Hixon.

Lothridge went on to Georgia Tech under legendary coach Bobby Dodd and was the most versatile player ever during Dodd's successful era.

Lothridge, who played quarterback, passed, ran, punted, placekicked, kicked off and played defense during his career at Georgia Tech, made All-America and was second to Navy's Roger Staubach in Heisman Trophy voting in 1963.

No big-time college football player has performed with as many different skills since the Lothridge days.

Lothridge went on to the National Football League with the Dallas Cowboys, Atlanta Falcons and Miami Dolphins.

He was backup quarterback to Don Meredith for a season at Dallas, but played most of his career with the Falcons where he twice led the NFL in punting and at times played defensive back.

But he is best remembered for his great days at Georgia Tech where he performed more football duties than any player since.

Dodd, himself a versatile All-American in his playing days at Tennessee, often said Lothridge was the best all-around college football player he ever saw.

Specialists have long since taken over in college football.

So, there is no doubt, Billy Lothridge was the last Billy Lothridge.

The ultimate over achiever

June 27, 1996

If any individual ever overdid the old "local boy makes good" syndrome, it has to be Gainesville native Reginald Murphy.

It was recently announced that Reg Murphy (we always called him Reginald when he was growing up on Oak Street in Gainesville some 50 years ago) has been named president and chief executive officer of the 108-year-old National Geographic Society.

Just how big is Murphy's big position?

The non-profit National Geographic Society, founded by Alexander Graham Bell, has nine million members, 40 million readers per magazine issue, 45 million television viewers and has published several million books.

Murphy's latest position is just another in a long line of big jobs he has held.

Murphy was best known in his younger days as a football and baseball player at Gainesville High School.

He was not a multi-talented star athlete, but he got the job done because he was a grinder, an old-fashioned hard worker who doggedly dedicated himself to any task he undertook.

Murphy's first professional success came in the newspaper business. He started out in journalism with Gainesville High's student newspaper, *The Trumpeter.*

He went to Mercer University, worked for the *Macon Telegraph,* the *Atlanta Constitution, Atlanta Magazine* and then back to the *Constitution* in editorial positions.

Murphy made national news in 1974 when he was kidnapped and held for 49 hours before the *Constitution* paid a $700,000 ransom.

The kidnapper was caught and later twice-convicted, the *Constitution* got its money back and Murphy went on to higher and higher journalistic positions such as editor and publisher of the *San Francisco Examiner* and similar positions with the *Baltimore Sun*.

Since there were apparently no higher executive rungs in journalism, Murphy got involved in golf administration and went on to serve two years as president of the United States Golf Association, the highest position in the world of golf.

And now Murphy is the big dog of the huge National Geographic Society.

But I'll just bet that back when Reginald was a kid on Oak Street, he had to sneak just to look at a copy of *National Geographic* Magazine because of those many pictures of scantily-clad native women.

CHAPTER 4

THE BIG DOGS CAME TO US, AND SOME WERE BRED HERE

Down through the years, some of the top sports figures in the world, for one reason or another, found their way to the Gainesville area. And some of the best got their start

Bud and The Boys

February 19, 1956

There is no doubt in the minds of at least 500 persons as to why Bud Wilkinson is a successful coach and leader.

These 500 fortunate individuals sat spellbound Friday night and listened with intense concentration while this tall, dignified young fellow from Oklahoma tempered quiet modesty, and intelligence with humor as he informally spoke of football, its contribution and its goal.

He touched on such things as "mental toughness," being satisfied with a personal effort and not merely the outcome, the will to succeed and the setting and ultimate accomplishment of a personal goal.

As Wilkinson talked, it seemed unimportant that he was the coach of a national championship team and was speaking at the Gainesville Touchdown Club's annual Jamboree.

The importance came with the realization that winning coaches, winning teams, touchdown clubs and even jamborees are all designed to instruct our youth in mental toughness, reaching a goal and being able to accept the setbacks.

Wilkinson's hypnotic delivery and smooth conveyance of thought almost, but not quite, overshadowed words spoken earlier by Dr. Ed Shannon who presented a talk on the history and accomplishments of the local TD group.

Shannon related the fact that the Gainesville Touchdowners were originated for the purpose of guiding our youth through the use of organized Little League and Midget Football programs.

The personable optometrist quoted a large monetary figure which had gone into the development of the program, money derived mostly from $20 membership fees paid by those in attendance.

Shannon emphasized the fact that members of the Touchdown Club were not required to be athletes, coaches or even sports fans. These men must only be interested in the future of boys. Gainesville's low rate of juvenile delinquency points up the importance of such a program.

All it takes to help improve this fine program, according to the good doctor, is "a love of boys and 20 bucks."

...JAMBOREE JABBER

Edd Travis, who guided the TD Club through this banner year, turned the president's gavel over to Drane Watson who handled the introduction of numerous visitors...C. V. Nalley was credited with securing Wilkinson's services for the Jamboree...Other members who were instrumental in the success program were Dewey Kephart, Charlie Hubbard, Charley Hearn, Charlie Edmondson, W. A. Crowe, George Van Giesen and Jim West...The Sooner coach was introduced to the packed house by Edwin Pope, executive sports editor of the *Atlanta Journal*...High school coaches on the scene were Owen Harris of Canton, Red Boyd of Toccoa, W. J. Askew of Monroe, Gene Alexander of South Habersham and Bill Collins of McDonough...Gainesville mentor Graham Hixon attended along with assistants Bobby Gruhn and Billy Beale...Coaching staffs from Georgia and Georgia Tech were well represented. Yellow Jackets present were Joe Pittard, Frank Broyles, Jack Griffin and John R. Bell. Bulldogs were Spec Towns, Perron Shoemaker, Sam Richwine, John Rauch, Quinton Lumpkin, Sterling Dupree and Bill Hartman... President Travis recognized Ray Knickerbocker and Glenn Gilreath for their work with the midget footballers and Little Leaguers.

When Little speaks, listen

January 14, 1958

Coaching great Lou Little—his voice husky with laryngitis but strong with the diction and delivery of a Shakespearean actor—spoke impressively to the Gainesville Touchdown Club here last night on football's past and present, its changes, problems and rewards.

As a large gathering listened intently, the scholarly Coach Little eloquently expounded facts, memories and observations that he has acquired through 52 years of direct association with the game of football.

During a question and answer session following the main talk, Little gave his opinions on the recent extra point rule change which makes it possible for teams to score two points on the conversion if the play is a run or a pass.

Little said he thought the rule makers should have gone a step further and moved the goal posts up to the goal line so that field goal attempts would be easier and more frequent. He said he did not know if the change would be good or bad until he saw it in action. But he had stated earlier in the evening that every rule change he had seen come about previously had all been for the best.

Little observed that the change puts the burden of a tough decision on coaches during a close game.

While still on the subject of rules, the retired coach said he was in favor of a common set of rules for the nation's high schools and colleges.

Remarking that he was in favor of free substitution, Little stated: "You can't write a ruling that makes a weak team strong or a strong team weak."

In comparing the early days of football with the game of today, Little said the present game is "far superior." He called the old game "stereotyped and dull" which has now developed into a contest with "color and imagination."

He called the 1957 season the "greatest in the history of the game" due to the number of upsets that brought on a "healthy condition."

"I like to see the unexpected," the dapper gentleman stated. "And long as the unexpected exists, the game will thrive."

Always an advocate of high scholastic standards for his players, Little said the increasing college enrollments will now raise these standards.

He urged high school coaches and parents to make sure their boys—whether football players or not—have the scholastic background to develop as students and citizens.

Little expressed a belief that coaches in the secondary or high schools do the best and hardest jobs in the game because they work with a boy at his early development stage.

We hope that Coach Little always exerts influence upon the game of football. Men of his type are priceless and can never be fully replaced.

As long as those of his breed are around to keep an intelligent eye on things, the game will accomplish the goals for which it was intended.

Red Sanders and RMA

August 15, 1958

Henry "Red" Sanders, an acknowledged coaching genius who enjoyed some great football years while at Riverside Military Academy here, died of a heart attack in Los Angeles yesterday.

Sanders was head coach at UCLA and had already established an outstanding record as a college head mentor at the time of his death, but Gainesville football fans will probably remember him best for the fine Blue Battalion teams he turned out in the years 1934–39.

Sanders' teams were so good in those days that Riverside was forced to compete with teams on college freshman and junior college levels. Riverside went all-out for football and Sanders made an outstanding mark here.

When he moved on to the college ranks and eventually became head coach at Vanderbilt University, he was influential in recruiting a young Gainesvillian named Bucky Curtis, son of Col. E. J. Curtis who is still athletic director at Riverside.

Sanders left Vanderbilt before Curtis completed his playing days, but Bucky went on to All-American fame and many gave the credit to Sanders.

He also is credited with the development of one Tommy Prothro who is now head coach at Oregon State. Prothro, son of ex-Southern League manager Doc Prothro, played under Red at Riverside and then joined him as an assistant at Vanderbilt and UCLA.

Sanders' over-all record as a collegiate coach was 102 wins, 41 losses and three ties.

Sanders was truly a great coach and they may claim him at Vanderbilt and UCLA, but the folks at Riverside will always lay the deepest claim to the man who believed in the teachings of football and swore by the single-wing.

Trippi talks

October 28, 1958

Charley Trippi, a human machine who once played football as if he invented it, talked of his game easily and informally to the Gainesville Touchdown Club here last night.

Bearing a smile left over from Georgia's 28-0 victory over Kentucky, the Bulldog assistant coach readily answered queries from the TD membership on his team, rule changes, so-called "dirty" play in the professional ranks and the game in general.

When asked how he compared Big 10 and Southeastern Conference football, Trippi minced no words. He called the Big 10 "overrated" due to a better "selling" job by the Midwesterners.

"They certainly have some good individual teams up there," he stated. "But your best football players come from the Southeast and the Southwest. The conferences are better balanced with more good teams. Professional rosters show where the better players hail from."

Trippi, although he once had his features altered while playing with the Chicago Cardinals, denied that pro football was dirty. "Both pro and college players sometime become over-aggressive," he said, "but I played seven years of professional football and I would not call it dirty."

Staying in line with many coaches, Trippi said he was against the new two-point conversion rule unless the goal posts were moved up to the goal line.

On the Bulldogs, Trippi remarked that they "needed" the win over Kentucky and that he looked for more solid play through the remainder of the season.

Glenn Gilreath, former football captain at Furman and now Little League chairman for the TD Club, best expressed Trippi's ability as a football player.

Said Gilreath: "I once played 60 minutes of football against Trippi and this is as close as I have ever been to him."

61

Joe DiMaggio talks of lengthy games, third major league during visit here

November 21, 1958

Joe DiMaggio (left), former New York Yankee great, talks with sportswriter Phil Jackson during a 1958 conversation in the lobby of Gainesville's Dixie Hunt Hotel. DiMaggio, at the time a public relations representative for a poultry foods concern, was in town visiting local poultry plants on behalf of his company.

Joe DiMaggio, looking as if he could still pound a baseball out of any park, talked rapidly and completely on some of the major problems facing the national pastime as he visited briefly here yesterday.

The tall, friendly gentleman—who could not be mistaken for anything other than a great athlete—easily handled the combined chores of signing autographs, making tape recordings and shaking hands as he answered questions in the lobby of the Dixie Hunt Hotel.

The man they dubbed "Joltin' Joe" and the "Yankee Clipper" would not criticize the game that transformed him from the unknown son of a modest, fisherman to an international figure, but he readily talked of baseball's problems.

"During my early days in baseball, a game seldom lasted more than two hours," he emphasized as he struggled with a ball-point pen that refused to write on the cover of a baseball which had been shoved into his hands.

"I think the long, drawn-out games of today certainly contribute to a lagging interest in the game. This has been partially caused by 'platoon baseball' which so many of the managers are playing."

"They use more pitchers in an average game today and are constantly substituting specialists. These moves tend to slow down play and make for long games. There seems to be a trend toward this sort of thing, but I think something should be done to speed up the average game."

On the subject of a proposed third major league, DiMag said seriously: "I don't believe there are enough good ballplayers at the present to furnish an additional 200 players that would be needed for a third league."

"The reason for this is the bad condition of the minor leagues. With so many leagues folding in the minors due to financial difficulties, there are not enough players being trained to man a third major league."

"I certainly think the majors should do all they can to solve the minor league problems. They should subsidize them and get them back on a sound basis. After all, the majors must draw their talent from the lower leagues."

He would not state that there were some players now performing in the majors that were not of major league caliber.

DiMaggio, now vice president in charge of trade relations for the V. H. Monette Co., a food brokerage firm, was in Gainesville touring the facilities of J. D. Jewell, Inc. The Monette Co. buys products from the Jewell organization for distribution to military outlets.

Dietzel on being right

January 13, 1959

Success as a football coach is a funny thing. It doesn't necessarily change a man's philosophy of coaching, but it does give him a chance to pass it on to others so they might benefit from it.

Coach Paul Dietzel, calm and confident as a young teacher lecturing to his class, talked warmly to the Gainesville Touchdown Club's Jamboree banquet here last night and his ideas should rank right along with his Louisiana State football team—at the top.

Had Paul Dietzel experienced a mediocre or losing record, he might have spent the banquet season listening instead of talking. As a loser, his ideas would have been the same, but cold human nature usually measures a man by his success in a given field. The fact that Dietzel is a winner accentuates the importance of his formula.

Said young Dietzel: "Convince yourself that you are right. Build yourself a good foundation and take your time in carrying it on. You might get fired in the process, but you can't consider what people might say. You've got to believe in yourself and you've got to be right."

Dietzel's success in building a national champion might be construed as proof that he was "right." But with him, his philosophy goes deeper than that.

"We have got to be right because we are molding boys into men," he emphasized. The young coach of the year admitted that he believes there is no substitute for victory. But while teaching this, he apparently has not forgotten an even greater responsibility to the overall development of the players who will at one time show the results of his influence.

According to his words, Dietzel never asked his team for perfection. He merely wanted an all-out effort. "I don't care how many mistakes you make," he instructed his boys, "just so you make them at full speed. It is no sin to make mistakes while attempting to attain a goal. The sin is aiming your sights too low."

Confidence was apparently the keynote to LSU's accomplishments. In speaking of the Chinese Bandits—a group of third-stringers who gained national renown because they refused to play like third-stringers—Dietzel smiled: "They thought they were good and I never bothered to tell them they weren't."

Dietzel gave full credit for his football knowledge to three great coaches with whom he has worked; Sid Gillman of the Los Angeles Rams, Red Blaik of Army and Bear Bryant of Alabama.

But his basic philosophy is his own. He says "you've got to be right," and after hearing him express his beliefs, we believe he is.

According to Howard

October 13, 1959

Clemson Coach Frank Howard, the humorous country gentleman from Barlow Bend, Ala., entertained the Gainesville Touchdown Club here last night with his famed collection of football tales in a southern drawl thick as molasses.

Some 300 persons laughed heartily as Howard's slow words covered everything from his playing days at Alabama to space travel.

According to Frank Howard....

"I didn't play football at Auburn because there was no NCAA in those days so Auburn didn't have much of a team."

"That Paul Dietzel out at LSU is a pretty little coach. He's like South Carolina's Warren 'Greezy.' They look like they haven't shaved yet."

"The main reason they invited my team to the Sugar Bowl last year was because the New Orleans folks were tired of having those Mississippi people there every New Years. They said all them folks had with them was a $10 bill and the 10 Commandments and didn't break either one."

"They play real wide-open football at South Carolina. It's nothing to see them run a quarterback sneak on third down and 18 yards to go."

"Georgia Tech is the best team I've seen this year. They ran only two plays against us, a sweep right and a sweep left. Of course, that's all they needed.

"The things I'd like to see in college football are (1) tryouts for high school players who are prospects; (2) one set of rules for all football; (3) foam-rubber coverings for plastic headgears and shoulder pads to keep down injuries; (4) national grant-in-aid rules; (5) a national TV day that would have the times of the bowl games staggered so you could see all of them.

"Most coaches know just about the same amount of football. Winning just depends on who gets the best boys."

"Bear down on your books boys because the entrance exams are getting tougher all the time. All the emphasis is being put on science and nuclear physics these days but there will still be a place for athletes and competitors, for if we ever get to the moon, we're probably going to have to fight somebody for it."

"I like a defensive end who performs like he's playing cards. One that charges into the backfield, grabs everybody up and shuffles through them. When he comes up with the man who has the ball, he keeps him."

BANQUET BANTER—Gainesville High Coach Graham Hixon introduced his Red Elephants and members of the coaching staff...Ed Nivens and Clayton Deavers presented reports on the progress of the club's Little League baseball and midget football programs...Among the guests was Pete Osborne of Cleveland whose son, Ronnie, is a 275-pound lineman at Clemson...University of Georgia assistant Quinton Lumpkin was on hand...TD Club president Washie Wallis presided over the meeting and Drane Watson introduced Howard...Charlie Simons thanked the speaker and presented him with a toy Clemson Tiger.

The last image

July 20, 1961

Ty Cobb, the man who could play the game of baseball better than any athlete who ever lived, was laid to rest in his hometown of Royston yesterday after thousands of written and spoken words had paid him spectacular and deserved tribute.

Many who know the Georgia Peach claim that Ty Cobb was Ty Cobb from the time he was born in the North Georgia hills until he died at the age of 74 in an Emory University Hospital bed last Monday afternoon.

Gainesville oldtimers Hyman Richardson and Ray Owens recall seeing Cobb play here with a Royston town team before he ever became a baseball great. "Ty was a frail youngster and just another pretty good player at that time," Richardson said. "But he could run then and he already had that competitive fire which eventually made him the greatest."

Richardson recalled that Cobb was on second base during a Royston-Gainesville game here and a heckler behind third base was using a megaphone to razz the visitors.

"Somebody got a hit," Richardson smiled, "and Cobb headed for home. As he rounded third, he threw a handful of dirt right down the mouth of that megaphone and the fellow almost choked to death."

Owens said he saw Cobb play only once, but he remembered it well, "Cobb has credit for a lot of stolen bases," Owens said, "but he didn't steal bases, he just TOOK them."

This type appraisal of Cobb's swashbuckling style of play lasted through more than 20 years in the major leagues. It endeared him to some but also made him many enemies.

Even in his late years, the fire in Cobb hadn't burned out. He was once asked what he thought about modern baseball and replied: "Nothing means much today. Some second rate rinky-dink can come up and pop a ball clear to the fence, a hit that with the old dead ball would have barely got out the infield."

Quotes such as this did little to endear him to the moderns, and it told the old ones that Cobb was still Cobb.

Many of the stories which have appeared during the past few days have pictured Cobb as a lonely man who was too busy being the best during his playing days to establish many close friends from the playing ranks.

The words told of his illness which greatly reduced his once robust, tough body.

I never saw Cobb play, but somehow I don't like this word picture of a lonely old man walking slowly and sadly into eternity while admirers grieve. This isn't Cobb and I don't think he would like it either.

66

The last image of the Georgia Peach I'll retain will show him sliding recklessly through the Pearly Gates, bandishing a handful of stardust and daring St. Peter to apply a tag.

Choo Choo chats

October 23, 1962

Charlie Justice, the fabulous former All-America tailback from North Carolina, talked to the Gainesville Touchdown Club here last night in a style similar to the way he once ran with a football—wide open, aggressive and highly entertaining.

Looking as if he could still elude a tackler or two despite a few extra pounds, the man they call "Choo Choo" was outspoken in voicing his dislike for those who advocate the deemphasis of college football and defended the game with personal examples of its worth.

"Football provided me with an education, a name and a living," said he. "If it hadn't been for football, I probably would never even have gone to high school. I'd have been a bum. Many people refer to football players and others connected with the game as bums. Yes, there are tramps and bums in football, but there are tramps and bums in any profession you name. There are no more of them in football than anywhere else."

But Justice was at his best recounting some of his playing experiences. He learned the value of blockers in a very unusual way. It was 1943 and he had just completed a fantastic high school career in Asheville, N.C. He was in the Navy and had made the Bainbridge Naval Base team along with a number of college and professional stars.

"I really thought I was a hotshot," he recalled with a smile. "In one game against Camp LeJuene I got off on a good run and had only one defender between me and the goal. Out front to block for me was Buster Ramsey who had been an All-American guard in college. But I figured I could do it all myself, so I cut away from behind Buster and tried to outrun the defender. I got tackled on the 15 yard line and before I could get off the ground, I felt someone grab me by the seat of the pants and the back of the neck and lift me off the ground. It was Ramsey."

"He turned me around to face him and said, 'Listen, you little high school so-and-so, you may think you know it all but I like to block just as well as you like to run. You just made a fool out of me in front of all these people and if you ever do it again I'll kill you'." With that, Ramsey tossed Justice to the ground.

"From that time on," Justice said, "I tried to use every blocker I could and I believe that was the key to my success."

Justice remembered playing for his high school team against Boys High of Atlanta in 1942. "On that day," said Choo Choo seriously, "I saw the fellow I believe to be the greatest football player ever. His name was Clint Castleberry. I'll never forget Castleberry or a fellow I played against at Georgia, Charlie Trippi." Justice said his first football idol was Frankie Sinkwich of Georgia.

In answer to a question concerning Tennessee's lack of success this season and attacks on the use of the single-wing, Justice—who ran from the single-wing at North Carolina—said he believed the formation still had a place in college football. "I see very little difference in it and the T-formation. The single-wing is not the trouble at Tennessee. They just don't have the horses to run it."

On the sudden success of his old pro team—the Washington Redskins—Justice credited the addition of Negro halfback Bobby Mitchell, a change in owner George Preston Marshal and additional experience of players and coaches.

"Mitchell has certainly helped the Redskins. George Marshal has turned all the coaching and trading over to Coach Bill McPeak. I believe Marshal also must have changed his attitude toward the use of Negro players. Last year, the coach and many of his players were rookies. They have all improved."

Charlie Justice said many more things and all of it was interesting. Add Choo Choo's names to the list of sports celebrities who have endeared themselves to Gainesville Touchdown Club members.

No promises, just work

January 16, 1964

Firm Joel Eaves and calm Vince Dooley addressed some 500 persons at the Gainesville Touchdown Club Jamboree here last night and made only one promise to University of Georgia supporters.

Eaves, Georgia's new athletic director, and Dooley, the young man who has assumed control of Bulldog football fortunes, made no glowing predictions of instant sports success at Georgia, but they impressed the cheering audience with their dignity, intelligence and a single pledge of hard work.

"We will work at winning," was the theme of short talks given by both men. Bulldog fans, long hungry for something to cheer about, responded with enthusiasm each time either man uttered the word "win."

Many remarks have been passed concerning the fact that Eaves, Dooley and most members of the new coaching staff at Georgia have Auburn backgrounds. "We've been kidded a lot about this War Dog and Bull Eagle thing," smiled the white-haired Eaves. "But I don't care what they call us so long as we win."

Said Dooley: "I'm certainly not ashamed of being from Auburn, but I'm a Bulldog now and I'm going to strive to be the best Bulldog ever."

An outstanding student and athlete at Auburn, Dooley said one aim of him and his staff is to make athletics and academics walk hand-in-hand at Georgia. The calm, confident type, Dooley communicated with the audience through old-fashioned common sense.

"So far as winning is concerned, I don't go along with all this talk about bad luck," Dooley said. "Of course, there is always that chance of the unexpected occurring, but I believe preparation is the key to winning. And when preparation meets opportunity, there is success."

It is plain that Eaves and Dooley are the type men any college would be glad to have representing its athletic department. No one should expect a sudden miracle at Georgia, but I firmly believe the new breed will eventually accomplish what bulldog folks have wanted for so long.

JAMBOREE JOTTINGS—Accompanying Eaves and Dooley were assistant coaches Mike Castronis, Frank Inman, Ken Cooper, Doc Ayers, Trainer Dick Copas and publicist Dan Magill...Eaves was introduced by Bill Bradshaw, Canton poultryman and former Georgia center...Out-going president Jack Short presided over the gathering and Gordon Sawyer was named new president. Short will serve as vice president, Jim Bates remains as secretary-treasurer and directors will be Ray Burch, Gene Fuller, Pug Fulenwider, Tommy Sheffield and Al MacMillan...Gainesville's Preston Ridlehuber was on hand with Bulldog teammates Ray Rismiller, Bob Taylor and Frank Lanckewicz...Esco Shaw, Walt Snelling and numerous volunteer coaches were recognized for their work with TD Club-sponsored Little League baseball and midget football. More than 700 boys took part in these programs during the year...Former Georgia coach Harry Mehre good-naturedly warned the new coaches about Georgia alumni...Both Eaves and Dooley received standing ovations from the large crowd.

Who stole Roger Staubach's hub caps?

February 28, 1966

Was it a three-year-old curse or just a coincidence that struck Roger Staubach when he came to Gainesville recently?

Staubach, Heisman Trophy winner and All-America quarterback for the U.S. Naval Academy in 1963, edged out Gainesville's Billy Lothridge, a Georgia Tech All-American, in the Heisman balloting that year.

Now serving his military obligation, Staubach is stationed at the Naval Supply School in nearby Athens and last weekend traveled to Gainesville to play with his supply school basketball team in a recreation tournament at the Gainesville High School gym.

While Staubach was taking part in the tournament, someone stole the hub caps from his car parked outside the gym.

It is not unusual for anyone's hub caps to be stolen anywhere these days.

However, it does seem highly coincidental in the first place that Staubach would end up playing basketball in the hometown of the fellow he beat out in the Heisman voting.

And it seems even more unusual that he would have his hub caps stolen.

Lothridge, now playing in the National Football League with the Atlanta Falcons, doesn't live in Gainesville these days and says he knows nothing about any hub caps.

The theft remains a great coincidental mystery.

The night Carnera was here

June 30, 1967

The towering man with a toothy grin rose heavily from a bench in the dank basement of the Gainesville Civic Building. He tugged at a pair of green wrestling trunks and stuck an oversized hand toward a young, skinny sports writer who stood in the doorway of the dressing room.

As the two shook hands, the massive paw of Primo Carnera enveloped the reporter almost to his elbow. "Ah, you are so young to be writer," Carnera said with his Italian accent and friendly but craggy smile. "In this time, not so many writers come to talk to me anymore. But I can understand. They now have more important people to write about." He didn't say it with any bitterness. He said it with the knowledge that everyone must face the hard facts of fleeting fame.

The year was sometime in the late 1940's. I can't remember exactly when. I only remember that Primo Carnera, the huge fellow they called the "gentle giant," was in Gainesville for a one-night wrestling stop. The glory of his boxing career was years behind him, and he was just another smalltime

70

wrestler picking up a few bucks by horsing around in rickety rings at count-less towns across the nation.

His appearance here was recalled when he died yesterday in the tiny Italian town of Sequals where he was born. Cancer cut down his once power-ful body on the 34th anniversary of his winning the world's heavyweight championship from Jack Sharkey. Death came at age 60.

Carnera started out to be a carpenter but turned to carnival perfor-mances and fighting because of his great size and strength. In his prime, he stood almost 6-5 and weighed 260 pounds. He won the heavyweight title by knocking out Sharkey in the sixth round in New York City on June 29, 1933. He lost it to Max Baer in 11 rounds June 14, 1934, after being knocked down 10 times.

He had a reputation for being able to withstand terrible punishment in the ring. However, this ability did not include hard licks to his "glass jaw," according to boxing lore. He fought some after the Baer knockout, but he never regained his previous form. He lost his last fight on November 21, 1945, by a knockout in the seventh by Luigi Musini in Milan, Italy. In 17 years in the ring, he had 100 fights, winning 66 by knockouts and 18 by decision.

During and after his tenure in the ring, his critics called him everything from a freak to a phony. Because of his gentle nature, he withstood these ver-bal attacks just as he did the physical blows.

He was past 40 when he climbed into the Civic Building ring here. It was rather a sad sight to see him going through the professional wrestling motions, clumsily clowning a bit and grimacing some when the script called for it. The usual loud-mouths who seem to appear in almost every wrestling crowd worked him over pretty well with catcalls and boos, but he took it without a single show of emotion.

If he had wanted to, he could have crushed every skull in the audience. I found myself almost wishing he would.

But as I remember my brief association with him, I know such a violent thought never crossed his mind. He was not a man of great intelligence, but he knew what was going on and accepted it. To me, Primo Carnera will always be a friendly, kind, overgrown guy who should have been a carpenter.

Tommy talks to kids

September 23, 1968

Tommy Nobis, the Atlanta Falcons linebacker whose mere presence sends National Football League ballcarriers into the nervous jerks, talked like

71

anything but a tough guy as he addressed more than 350 persons attending the Gainesville Touchdown Club meeting at the Civic Center here last night.

Speaking in fluent Texan and built like a red-headed cornerstone, Nobis directed most of his remarks to the young boys in the audience, and his advice was as solid as one of his resounding tackles.

He said most of the things other speakers say to youngsters. He talked about staying with the books, building good habits in studying and athletics, having faith and paying attention to people who are trying to help.

When such words are uttered by more glib speakers, they sometimes tend to sound a bit corny or too slick. But Nobis delivered them with naturalness and sincerity.

From seeing him perform, I have always respected Nobis as a dedicated athlete. Now I respect him even more. Not merely because of what he said to those kids, but the way he said it. You could tell he meant and believed every word.

When touching on the fortunes of the Falcons, Tommy displayed both a sense of humor and a belief in the future.

"I was going to bring a Falcons highlights film along," he laughed. "But they're still trying to put one together."

He believes the Atlanta team is near to being a bonafide competitor in the NFL. "We are just inches away," he said as he demonstrated with two thick fingers held up close together.

"We may be just one game away. Maybe even just a half or one play. We just need a little unity and we will be okay."

Nobis pointed out that 11 of the Falcons now playing regularly were not even with the team during pre-season training.

"We are struggling along right now," he said. "But when we get to know each other better, I believe we have the talent to be a good team."

Hitting at some of the criticisms of the Falcons, Nobis said emphatically: "A new head coach or new owner certainly isn't the answer. We just all have to work harder and everyone has to do his part. I hate to think there are players in pro football who don't have the desire to put out for four quarters. I don't think we have any."

In closing, Nobis said he believed in the future of the Falcons and hopes there was a place for him in their plans.

Leaping longhorns, Tommy! If there ain't a place for you in the Falcons future, the whole flappin' franchise is in trouble!

BANQUET BANTER—TD Club president Jim West recognized coaches and some players in the National Little League and Pony League baseball programs and junior high and midget football leagues...Membership Chairman Joe Stargel announced that the club now has 426 members and the goal of 500 is expected soon...Nobis was introduced by Bill White, program chairman. Response was made by Preston Ridlehuber, a former teammate of Nobis with the Falcons...During a question and answer session, Nobis praised Gainesville's Billy Martin who is now with the Minnesota Vikings. Tommy said Martin had a lot to do with the Vikings' win over Atlanta in the season opener and pointed out that the Jolly Giant was not only a fine player but also a big morale factor when he was with the Falcons...Billy's Minnesota teammates presented him with the game ball after the win over Atlanta.

A double Mickey

June 14, 1969

When former New York Yankee great Mickey Mantle visited Gainesville recently, he came here to watch Mickey Mantle play centerfield.

The unique situation came about when superstar Mantle visited Riverside Military Academy and was a spectator when his son, Mickey Mantle Jr., played on the Riverside baseball team.

During his brief visit, the elder Mantle said he sent his son to Riverside to get him away from the pestering he gets back home in Dallas, Tex., because his father is the idol of millions.

When he came to Riverside, young Mantle wasn't planning to play baseball, said Pedro Vidal, the Riverside coach. "But I talked him into it. He wanted to pitch, but we put him in centerfield. He's a fine boy and a good player. We're glad to have him."

A sophomore, young Mantle hit near .300 for the season and was named honorable mention All Mid-South Conference along with teammates Serigo Molina at second base and G. R. Rodriguez at shortstop.

Young Mantle's presence at Riverside made it possible for umpire James B. Clegg to enjoy a unique experience.

Clegg, principal of Chestatee School in Forsyth County, umpired in games involving both Mantles.

For several years, Clegg umpired in the old Class AAA American Association. In July of 1952, the Yankees sent a strong young player named Mickey Mantle to their Kansas City farm team where he rapped the ball so hard for 40 games that he was recalled to the parent club where he embarked on a brilliant major league career.

Clegg umpired several of those games.

This past April, 18 years after he umpired for the original Mickey, Clegg called a game between Riverside and McCallie at the Riverside field.

Playing centerfield for Riverside was Mickey Mantle Jr. Probably no other umpire had the double Mickey experience.

Prothro Riverside bred

January 24, 1971

Coach Tommy Prothro, former national collegiate coach of the year, has left the college ranks to become head coach of the Los Angeles Rams of the National Football League.

A product of Gainesville's Riverside Military Academy, Prothro was named college coach of the year in 1966 after his UCLA Bruins upset Michigan State in the Rose Bowl.

A 1938 graduate of Riverside, Prothro played end on the football team was All-Conference as a junior and All-Southern as a senior. He also played baseball and was high point man on the track team.

After graduation from Riverside, Prothro went on to Duke University and, after World War II service, he joined his old Riverside coach, Red Sanders, as an assistant at UCLA and later became head coach at Oregon State.

Mitchell and the kids

November 10, 1971

Jim Mitchell, the multi-talented tight end of the Atlanta Falcons proved here last night he is just as popular off the field as on when he appeared as featured guest of the South Hall Area Touchdown Club banquet before an overflow crowd of 476 persons at Holiday Inn.

Much of the audience was made up of youngsters who participate in the club's junior football leagues. Mitchell, a 230-pounder who may well be the best man at his position in all of professional football, was swamped by auto graph seekers before and after the event.

A question and answer session, which might have gone on all night had it not been halted, revealed some of Mitchell's insights into the pro game. During a Falcons highlights film which climaxed the evening, Mitchell's catches, runs and touchdowns brought cheers from the elementary set.

Accompanied by his wife Marjorie and tiny son Darrien, Mitchell answered various questions with the following personal opinions: Deacon Jones of the Los Angeles Rams and Dick Butkus of the Chicago Bears are the toughest men to block; John Brodie of San Francisco and Roman Gabriel of LA are the top quarterbacks; tight end is the most difficult position to play; the Falcons are going to win the Super Bowl over the Baltimore Colts; Coach Norm Van Brocklin is a fine guy except from Friday afternoon through Sunday; Tommy Nobis is the Falcons' best football player and is too tough to be shifted from linebacker to offensive center.

Mitchell, who starred at three different positions at Prairie View A&M before being drafted by the Falcons, said privately he thought he would be playing with the Houston Oilers because of their close proximity to his college, but admitted he is now very happy he ended up with the Falcons. "I like it so much, I'm in the process of buying a home in Atlanta," he said with a huge, congenial smile which belies his physical performance on the field.

If a poll had been taken here last night, Jim Mitchell would already be All-Pro by unanimous vote.

BANQUET BANTER—More than 400 boys took part this past season in the South Hall Area junior football program...Short talks were given by Clyde Cronic, Jr., president of the club, and Phil Carpenter, head coach of the South Hall Knights...Paul White was recognized as commissioner of the football leagues and Doug Casper as head of the baseball program...First place trophies in two leagues and the playoffs went to teams from Oakwood and Flowery Branch as Gainesville Mill, Flowery Branch and Oakwood took runner-up awards.

Super Lou

March 12, 1972

Lou Hudson of the Atlanta Hawks is a fellow who has made a lot of adjustments in his basketball career, and he made another one here Friday night when he spoke to more than 500 persons at the South Hall Area Club's basketball banquet at the Civic Center.

The tall, slender, articulate NBA shooting star and all-pro has seen the Hawks go from a championship team to a loser and has become accustomed to being shifted back and forth from guard to forward.

When he arrived at the Civic Center Friday night and noticed that much of the audience consisted of young elementary basketball players, both boys and girls, he was taken a bit by surprise.

"I didn't realize there was going to be so many children here," he said.

75

"I don't think the speech I had planned will be appropriate."

But once again Hudson adjusted, gave an interesting short talk about the Hawks and basketball in general and then took part in a question and answer session which might have gone on all night had it not been halted.

The kids asked Hudson everything from his shoe size to his middle name (which is Clyde), and he fielded the questions neatly with humor and patience.

Concerning the Hawks, Hudson attributes their lack of success to the fact the team is made up of so many players who never performed with each other before this season. "We still haven't learned all there is to know about each other," he said. "At times we look great and at times we are awful. But I believe with hard work we will get much better."

On Pete Maravich, Hudson thinks the Pistol will become a great NBA player, possibly by next season. "Pete is only in his second year in the league and he has had some physical problems. He still does some of the things he got away with in college, things that just won't work in the pros. But he's learning and I believe he will become a great player."

When asked if he would consider jumping to the rival ABA if "offered a bundle of money," Hudson replied: "I've already had such offers and I didn't jump. I haven't ever really considered playing with any other team."

The evening closed with the kids surrounding Hudson for autographs after they had given him a standing ovation.

They call him Super Lou Hudson when he plays, and he did a super job off the court here Friday night.

Ol' Diz

July 21, 1974

They buried Jay Herman (Dizzy) Dean yesterday near his hometown of Wiggins in south Mississippi, and with him went a very colorful hunk of baseball's past.

The son of an itinerant cotton picker, Dean literally powered his way into the baseball record books with an awesome fast ball that got him 30 victories in a single season and two World Series wins with the old St. Louis Cardinals' Gashouse Gang of 1934.

He was the superstar of his day. As a small boy in the mid 1930's, I can recall those smiling photos of ol' Diz in a seemingly always dirty and always wrinkled Cardinal uniform, with his baseball cap cocked to one side, and having a ball as he hammed it up for the cameramen.

Athletic stars of today didn't invent the commercial side of the game. Magazines in the 1930's were filled with cartoon ads showing Dizzy in street clothes, throwing a humming baseball a city block to knock down a gang of bank robbers and capture them for the police. The punch line of the strip always showed Dizzy holding up a box of Grapenuts Flakes and giving the cereal all the credit for his prowess.

I don't know how much money Dean got paid for such things, but it was effective. I never could stand the taste of that particular cereal, but I forced a few bowls of it down and waited for something magic to happen. Alas, it never helped my fast ball because every other kid in the neighborhood continued to belt it out of sight.

Fans who don't remember Dizzy's playing days can certainly recall his career as a baseball broadcaster for television when he worked with former Brooklyn Dodger Pee Wee Reese.

Dean was far from the slick, glib play-by-play announcers of the present. In fact, Dizzy was more of a "by-play" broadcaster. Many times he talked of almost everything but the game at hand.

He talked about old friends back home in Wiggins, hunting trips, past games, childhood memories, bird dogs, his brother Paul who pitched with him on the Cardinals, and he always had high praise for cold Falstaff beer, his sponsor at the time.

Most of the time, Dizzy talked about himself and his exploits as a pitcher. But he didn't come across boastful because he sounded so sincere with that backwoods drawl and homespun manner.

Although he was a great player, Dean's knowledge of the game was somewhat lacking when it came to broadcasting. He often got the teams confused, could pronounce only a few names correctly and his grammar was atrocious. But he was like Junior Samples of "Hee Haw" fame today. It wasn't a put-on. That was just the way Dizzy was and it endeared him to fans all over the nation.

The last time I saw Dizzy he was here to help dedicate a Woodmen of the World camp on Lake Lanier. I had an appointment to interview him at a local motel. But when I got there, Dizzy was too relaxed to talk. His trip had apparently fatigued him and he was resting with a brown bottle clutched tightly like a teddy bear.

I think a fitting epitaph for Dean would be the words to "The Wabash Cannonball," his favorite country classic that he would belt out while in the midst of a game broadcast.

I can hear that country twangy voice of his now:

"Listen to the jingle the rumble and the roar as she glides along the woodland by the hills and by the shore.

Here the mighty rush of the engine, hear the lonesome hoboe's squall
You're traveling through the jungles on the Wabash Cannonball."
I have often thought it was Dizzy's favorite song because he thought of
his fast ball roaring along like the Wabash Cannonball. Dean had a very high
opinion of himself as a pitcher and could never be accused of being modest.
Farewell, Dizzy. You made sports fun, and that's the way it should be.

Big win for Maxey's Truck Stop

March 30, 1977

The touching tears of Al McGuire have gone away, Marquette has prop-
erly enshrined its NCAA basketball championship trophy, North Carolina is
off somewhere standing in its four corners, and the Omni is once again a mis-
shapen building where the Hawks and Flames try not to lose too often.

The circus is over. Nevada-Las Vegas has gone to that big roulette wheel
in the sky and Cornbread Maxwell is back in Kinston, N.C., telling all the folks
how it was playing against the big boys.

It was amazing that McGuire, a character right out of a Damon Runyan
short story, occupied center ring from the day the big top opened until the last
piece of cotton candy melted into the sawdust.

In fact, they must have invented center rings for guys like McGuire.
Irreverent, snarling, playing to the crowd, guarding against coachlike quotes,
feigning deep anguish, cajoling his players and intimidating officials,
McGuire's act is vintage arena. You can't see his tongue in his cheek but it's
there. He's putting everybody on and making them love it.

In fact, McGuire was so relaxed during preparations for the Final Four
at Atlanta's Omni that he sneaked off for a couple of rounds of golf at
Gainesville's Chattahoochee Golf Course.

Marquette's national championship basketball team was a collection of
long arms and muscles which played defense with the desperation of a street
fighter backed up against an alley wall. There was nothing pretty about it.

Their shirttails hung out and they looked about as collegiate as a road
gang. Sometimes they played like Maxey's Truck Stop of the Coweta County
Recreation League. They cussed each other, shoved each other and argued
among themselves. They played the game as if the winners were going to split
a big keg of beer rather than receive a trophy from the high-sounding National
Collegiate Athletic Association.

There was no outward, misty-eyed dedication of that final game to
the good ol' Coach Al McGuire. It was more like they were playing hard

because the boss was about to be sent up the river for a long stretch in the big house.

Losers seven times in the regular season, the Warriors had to be the rag-tags of the final four. There was no charisma as in Carolina blue. There was no dash of the running Rebels from the wicked city of Las Vegas. There was no Charlotte aura of smalltownboy-makes-good. It was just Mean Man McGuire and a bunch of guys from over at the playground.

To the end, the Warriors were the have-nots. When it came time for the traditional removal of the nets, they didn't even own any scissors to cut them down. They ripped them off manually.

In the final moments of the championship game, the television cameras caught McGuire rubbing tears from his eyes. But that didn't last long. Like all tough guys in the movies, Al quickly got his emotions under control and once again became George Raft standing on a street corner, coolly flipping a silver dollar.

But I believe it would have been more fitting if they had plunged the Omni into darkness except for one spotlight on center court. McGuire could have walked out in Emmett Kelley attire, carrying a broom, and swept up that final spotlight with the soft strands of "Where Are the Clowns" playing in the background.

Mehre was well known here

September 28, 1978

Harry Mehre, former University of Georgia football coach and a familiar figure to many Gainesvillians, died at his Atlanta home yesterday of apparent heart failure.

A center for Notre Dame in the early 1920s and head football coach at Georgia and Ole Miss from 1928 to 1945, Mehre was 77 years old.

Mehre, starting center under Knute Rockne in 1921 and also an outstanding basketball player, went to Georgia as line coach in 1924 and became head coach there four years later. He switched to Ole Miss in 1938.

One of Mehre's most memorable teams at Georgia was in 1929 when a number of former Gainesville High School athletes played for him including Tom Paris Sr. and the late Bennie Rothstein. Mehre was also well known here as a humorous speaker at touchdown club and civic club meetings.

Mehre had only two losing seasons during his 10 years at Georgia. His record at Georgia was 59-34-6 and his eight-year record at Ole Miss was 39-26-1. After 18 years as a head coach, Mehre began a successful career as a soft drink wholesaler and also wrote as a football analyst for the *Atlanta Journal.*

Mehre had been in poor health for some time. He suffered a heart attack about five years ago and later had a stroke. He complained shortly after midnight about feeling ill and his wife had him lie down while she went to get him some water. When she returned, he was dead.

Mehre was the backup center at Notre Dame in George Glipp's final season (1920) and the "Four Horsemen" were freshmen in his final season when the Fighting Irish went 10-1 with only a 10-7 loss to Iowa blotting their record.

George Woodruff, then the head coach at Georgia, introduced the Notre Dame formation to the South in 1924, bringing in two Rockne disciples, Mehre and (backfield coach) Frank Thomas, who later had a brilliant career at Alabama.

Woodruff, a wealthy businessman who didn't want to continue coaching, retired after the 1927 season and Mehre moved up.

One of the highlights of Mehre's coaching career came in 1929 when a sophomore-dominated Georgia team upset then highly-regarded Yale, 15-0.

Mehre, noted for his wit, was in wide demand as a public speaker but retired from public life after his heart attack.

Billy, Tom T., Big Jawn and Whack
April 7, 1978

If you like name-dropping, you should have been hanging around the premises of the Holiday Inn here Saturday night.

I was on hand to attend the fourth annual Old Timers' Supper, a gathering of former Industrial League baseball and basketball players who performed in a range of years from the 1920's into the 1950's.

Prior to the event, I dropped by a place of libation known as the Hangar Four Lounge which had not yet attracted the usual Saturday night fevering.

But there was a small group there including a grinning, talkative fellow named Billy Carter who I understand has a brother who holds a rather important job in Washington, D.C. Billy's entourage also included country singer Tom T. Hall who was preparing himself for an appearance at the Gym of '36 here.

I didn't know the other guys in the party and didn't hang around long enough for any introductions.

Incidentally, Carter was drinking vodka. There was no Billy Beer on hand and he should be glad. That stuff tastes worse than low-grade canned heat.

Anyway, there were more celebrities present over at the old timers' gathering in the nearby Sky Room. Former major league slugging great Johnny Mize, a native of Demorest in Habersham County, and Whack Hyder, for 22 years the basketball coach at Georgia Tech and a native of the Lula-Clermont area, were there to reacquaint themselves with some old friends.

Some 130 athletes, from as far away as Texas and Mississippi, enjoyed a gala evening of fun and lie-telling at the gathering held each year by the Old Timers' Club.

Dub Jones, who once played baseball and basketball for New Holland and later coached some fine high school basketball teams at East Hall, served as the humorous master of ceremonies and anybody who wanted to got up to say a few words.

Another guest of honor was U.S. Congressman Ed Jenkins who is proud of the fact that he once played a bit of second base throughout various parts of the hill country.

Hyder, who was one of the few college coaches who could hold his own against Adolph Rupp's Kentucky powerhouses, had some kind words to say about his playing days and associations in these parts.

Said Hyder: "I see a lot of fellas here I thought were mean as hell when I played against them. I've found out since getting to know them, they're pretty good folks."

Mize, who doesn't care for public speaking, was enticed to say a few words and answer some questions about why he hasn't been voted into major league baseball's hall of fame.

"Big Jawn," as he was known in his home run days with the St. Louis Cardinals and later the New York Yankees, seems to think sportswriters shouldn't have so much of the voting power for spots in the hall of fame. I tend to agree with him.

Besides, despite his gray hair, Mize still looks strong enough to pump most sportswriters over a fence somewhere.

There were more inductees into the Blue Ridge Hall of Fame; one of them, Lamar Murphy, was named to the hall in both baseball and football. Other baseball selectees were Pete Morgan (also installed as the new president of the Old Timers' Club); Skinny Vaughn, Hugh Dorsey Campbell and the late Lee Crowe.

Those honored in basketball included Dean Evans, Dub Jones, Ralph Chapman, the late Sylvester Jones, James Barnes, B. C. Jarrard, Bob

81

Strickland, Ted Ivey, Ralph (Pee Wee) Smith, "Little" Ralph Smith, T. J. Chapman, June Boggs, Paul McDonald and Pokey Allen.

Getting back to name-dropping, you can't ask for more of a variety than Billy Carter's mouth, Tom T. Hall's singing, Johnny Mize's power and the gentlemaness of Whack Hyder.

CHAPTER 5

GAME OF GOLF AT THE HEART OF ACCOMPLISHMENT

Ranging from scruffy nine-hole courses to the royal emerald acres of the Masters, the game of golf spawned some big-time doings in these parts.

Hometown recognition biggest thrill

August 25, 1957

"This night is a bigger thrill to me than all my tournament victories combined."

So said a young Tommy Aaron Friday to Gainesville friends who gathered to honor him at the Avion Restaurant with a "Tommy Aaron Appreciation Dinner."

Aaron—who speaks softly but carries a big golf stick—was recognized for becoming Georgia's leading golfer by winning the Georgia Open, the Georgia Amateur and the Southeastern Conference championship.

The 20-year-old linksman voiced his humble thanks to the gathering of homefolks after being presented with a silver trophy by Charlie Yates on behalf of the Gainesville-Hall County Chamber of Commerce, sponsor of the event.

Yates, who in past years brought a host of golfing trophies back to Georgia and is currently non-playing captain of the Walker Cup team, gave the evening's featured address. He told the gathering that virtues displayed by Aaron on the course are the most important ones needed on everyday life.

Clayton Deavers, Aaron's high school football and basketball coach, told of Aaron's inspiring performances as a prep athlete. The same traits of leadership, confidence and concentration that Aaron displayed in high school have carried him on to his golfing victories, Deavers stated.

John Davis, secretary of the Chattahoochee Country Club, spoke on behalf of club president J. D. Jewell and presented Aaron with a lifetime membership to the club.

Chamber of Commerce President Claude Williams, Jr. and Dr. Ed Shannon presided over the gathering.

Williams read congratulatory messages from President Dwight Eisenhower, Governor Marvin Griffin, amateur great Billy Joe Patton and professional Ben Hogan and acknowledged receipt of many other messages from golfing notables all over the nation.

Charles Thurmond, Gainesville mayor pro-tem, read a proclamation by Mayor Ray Knickerbocker designating Friday as "Tommy Aaron Day" in Gainesville.

Aaron named to Walker Cup

February 1, 1959

Tommy Aaron, whose husky shoulders are broad enough to hold many golfing honors that have been heaped upon him, yesterday picked up one of the most treasured laurels that can be bestowed upon an amateur when he was named to the 1959 United States Walker Cup team.

The 21-year-old Gainesvillian will join eight other members of the team—America's best—and meet the British amateur stars in the 17th renewal of the biennial series at Muirfield, Scotland, next May 15–16.

When Aaron was asked here Saturday if he would be able to make the trip, he smiled and said with an accent: "Aye think aye'll make the trip to Scotland."

Aaron is a quiet young man who never bubbles with enthusiasm over any situation. But you could tell from his twinkling eyes that he was pleased as any small town youngster could be on being told that he would represent his country in international competition.

Tommy is one of four newcomers named to the squad. The others are Deane R. Beman, 20, Silver Springs, Md.; Jack Nicklaus, 19, Columbus, Ohio; and H. Wettlaufer, 23, of Buffalo, N. Y.

Charles Coe of Oklahoma City was chosen captain of the team which includes Bill Hyndman III of Abington, Pa.; Billy Joe Patton of Morganton, N. C.; Dr. Frank M. Taylor Jr., of Pomona, Calif., and Harvie Ward of San Francisco.

In the event that any of these players cannot make the trip to Scotland, alternates chosen were William Campbell of Huntington, W. Va.; Charles Kocsis of Royal Oak, Mich., and Dick Chapman of Pinehurst, N. C.

The team was selected by the United States Golf Association.

Aaron, who stormed through the National Amateur before finishing runner-up to Coe in the finals, has also been invited to play in the annual benefit exhibition match at North Fulton on March 29 which precedes the Masters Tournament.

In the exhibition, Aaron will be playing with the 1958 Masters winner Arnold Palmer. The rest of the playing group might include George Bayer, Patty Berg and Bing Crosby or Pat Boone.

Aaron climbed into the "big time" last year and found the company to his liking.

The Masters, Aaron's first

April 6, 1959

A collection of incidents that sticks in the mind after four days of watching the super-brilliant Masters Tournament:

Tommy Aaron's beautiful drive off the first tee opening day. His expertly played birdies on the tough par five second and 13th holes. The unthinking fans who called Aaron to the gallery for conversation and introductions while the youngster was lining up a hard putt, and the distraction caused him to four-putt the hole. Aaron's chest-out, drum major stride as he walked the plush fairways.

Talking with Gainesvillians such as Dr. Shelley Ellott, Oscar Lilly, Jim Warner, the Revs. James McRay and Richard Bates, Ed Shannon, Ray Godfrey, Jimmy Robinson, Julian Franklin, Jack Phillips, Bobby Lord, Bunk Sorrells, Jim Bates, Perrin Reynolds, Father Michael Manning, Wendall Jackson, Bill Carroll, Jean Wilson, Jimmye Foster, Mr. and Mrs. Charlie Aaron and many others.

Tommy's bashful grin as he signed autographs for eager youngsters.

The tremendous roar that went up from the thousands around the 18th green as Art Wall cupped the birdie putt that eventually meant victory.

Dr. Cary Middlecoff's great second shot that almost hit the pin on number 15 and led to an eagle on the hole.

Monstrous George Bayer hitting a booming driver and four-iron to within eight feet of the hole off the 475-yard 13th.

Billy Joe Patton's low, lining iron shot hit and stayed on top of a narrow retention dam near the rear of number 11 green that helped the colorful amateur get his par.

The tremendous galleries following Sammy Snead and Ben Hogan on Saturday and Middlecoff Sunday.

Professional John McMullin, like any weekend duffer, actually topping his drive just off the front of the tee on number 14.

Steady Stan Leonard's description of playing the scenic Augusta National course. "It's the most exacting course in the world. It tires you physically to walk it and wears you out mentally figuring how to play it. You must think, think and concentrate on every single shot."

Mike Souchak banging his club against a tree in disgust over a missed shot and later trying to straighten it out again with a steel stake.

The look of disbelief that swept over Chick Harbert's face after he missed a 12-inch putt.

The amazing way Arnold Palmer kept getting into trouble with bad shots and immediately recovering with great ones.

The caddies all predicting sub-par scores for their players.

The mink club covers used by Souchak and Doug Ford.

Hearing almost every spectator vowing to come back next year to watch what is possibly the most colorful sports show on earth.

Aaron clubs doubters

July 25, 1960

Tommy Aaron, the young Gainesville amateur who had to shoot a fabulous round of golf before receiving long over-due credit in his own state, has now won just about all there is to win in these parts and begins branching out next month.

Although outsiders might claim prejudice, Aaron has long been regarded in Gainesville as Georgia's finest amateur golfer since the great Bobby Jones. No other state linksman can even approach Aaron's record on a local, national or international basis.

Yet, it was not until he scored a fantastic 10-under-par 62 in the third round of the Georgia Amateur that he received the statewide newspaper recognition which he has so long deserved.

Up until he made a runaway of the state amateur, it didn't seem to matter that he was the only Georgia golfer ever to win both the Georgia Open and Georgia Amateur in the same year and the only amateur ever to take the Georgia Open, a feat he has twice accomplished.

The so-called experts also tended to overlook his charge to the National Amateur finals in 1958 and his selection to the victorious U.S. Walker Cup team. While national golfing publications were listing him among the top 10 amateur golfers in the country, some home-state experts were still apparently doubtful.

It appears that he had clubbed away that doubt. To go along with his state amateur victory this year, he has won the National Tournament of Club Champions, the Southeastern Amateur, led the way in a Southern Pro-Am threesome win and finished fourth among all amateurs in the great Masters Tournament.

Aaron is currently working on a sub-par streak. In his last 11 straight rounds of competitive golf, he has been below regulation figures.

Aaron is preparing for his biggest quest of the season. He will enter the highly-regarded Western Amateur which will be held August 1–7 at Northland Country Club in Duluth, Minn.

After that, he will try for a third Georgia Open crown and take another shot at the National Amateur at the St. Louis Country Club in Clayton, Mo.

If Aaron keeps his game at its present pitch, he can hardly miss bringing further laurels back to Gainesville.

Yes, there are golfers

May 22, 1960

Admitting immediately that I know nothing about politics and even less about large sums of money, I still feel obligated to aim a few words at a few uninformed folks who apparently know very little about the popularity of golf.

Some individuals in Gainesville, a couple of politicians included, have recently been engaged in sidewalk verbal attacks against the new municipal golf course. Their statements center around the money being spent on the course and what they refer to as the "few" number of golfers in the area.

These people have the right to oppose anything they wish, but their grounds for opposition here are entirely wrong. There are literally hundreds of individuals in and around Gainesville who participate in the game of golf.

For the past few years, many of these participants have been willing to travel to such places as Athens, Commerce, Toccoa, Atlanta, Canton and Skitts Mountain in order to take part in their chosen recreation. On many occasions, Gainesvillians playing on these courses outnumber the hometowners.

Another large group of golfers temporarily gave up the game when the old municipal course went under the waters of Lake Lanier. They either were not willing to undergo the travel or could not afford the extra expense. These folks are already talking of taking up the game once more when the new course is opened.

There is still another group waiting to take advantage of the facility. They are the beginners who have never played but now have their first opportunity and are planning to do so. A number of local ladies are currently engaged in weekly instruction classes.

Yes, there is yet another group. Last year more than 4,000,000 persons flocked from all points to frolic on Lake Lanier and more will come in future years. Many of these tourists are golfers and some of them will certainly take advantage of the presence of a course near the lake.

The above-mentioned groups do not include many of the people who currently don't seem to care one way or the other about the course. They, too, might succumb to the growing popularity of the game.

I can think of no more useful addition to our recreation facilities, and the entire project will be even more successful if the skeptics would help to promote the course rather than knock it.

There are those days

July 30, 1969

One of the unique things about the game of golf is that sometimes you strike the ball well but your score is not impressive. At other times, you can hardly keep the darn thing in play but still manage to come up with low numbers.

When you hear of a professional winning a major tournament, your mind conjures up an image of the guy stroking it beautifully down the middle, hitting everything to the green and sinking for birds and pars. This ain't necessarily so.

A case in point is Tommy Aaron's victory in the Canadian Open, especially his two-under-par 70 which beat Sam Snead in the 18-hole playoff Monday.

Aaron said himself after the round: "Overall I didn't feel I was playing too good. There have been a few times I've felt I played well enough to win, and didn't, so I guess my luck has changed."

Many times during the playoff, Aaron took the scenic route through maple trees which are prevalent on the course which bears the misleading name of Pinegrove.

Tommy whacked his tee shot into a grove of trees on the fifth but came out with a crowd-pleasing birdie by sinking a 70-foot putt. He bogied number 10 after his ball came to rest behind the green beside a tree, and bogied the 12th when he hit his shot 40 feet below the green in another clump of maples.

He toured through the maples again on 16 but salvaged his par with a deft chip shot. Actually, back at 12, he rammed in a 15-footer for the bogey.

This type of golf is commonly known as "scrambling," and most successful pros have to be good at it because it is humanly impossible for even the most talented swingers to keep the ball in easy play day after day and hole after hole. On the days when the pros aren't "sweet-shooting" it, they must become scramblers or forget about the pay window.

One thing is for sure, if they scramble successfully, the short game must be at its best, especially in the putting department.

Putting was the difference between Aaron and Snead Monday. Sam was longer and more accurate than Tommy on that particular day but the loser said to the winner when it was all over: "I'd like to borrow that putting stroke of yours for just one season."

Aaron has one of the most picturesque swings in all of golf. And yet, on the day of his first tournament victory, his greatest weapons were coolness, experience and the gentle touch of a pickpocket.

The hard way

May 22, 1970

Golf is not an easy game. In fact, it is probably the most difficult game there is to play well. But within the confines of the sport, there are degrees o. ways to go about coming up with desired low numbers.

It wasn't by choice, but Tommy Aaron shot a fine, four under par 68 the hard way in the opening round of the Atlanta Golf Classic yesterday.

There were many factors involved as the calm, slender Gainesvilliar stroked his way around the tight Atlanta Country Club course in intense heat.

First, the course played shorter because of the weather. Add to this the fact that Aaron was striking the ball extremely well most of the time. The log ical conclusion is that he would naturally have to shoot a good score.

However, because of the hard fairways, most of the leaders gained strokes on the par five holes which were easier to reach in two. Not Aaron. He had six birdies on the day and only one of them came on a par five.

We also have to consider the play and conduct of the other two members of Aaron's threesome, Charlie Sifford and Chi Chi Rodriguez. Many profes sional golfers will tell you that good or bad play is contagious. In other words there is a tendency to hit the ball in a similar fashion to those playing with you.

Not Aaron. While Sifford and Rodriguez were struggling and griping their way to a 75 and a 78, Tommy seemed to isolate himself and protect his game from infection.

Sifford is a 48-year-old who constantly chews on a cigar surrounded by a scowl. Rodriguez is a slightly-built Puerto Rican known for his clowning. No once did he go into his act yesterday.

Sifford and Rodriguez haven't been playing well lately. They didn't play well yesterday and their dispositions fit their performances perfectly.

Through all this, Aaron cooled it. He whacked some truly beautifu shots along the way. Consistently hitting the ball near the flagsticks, Tommy sank birdie putts of 12, 15 and four feet on par four holes on his first nine. Hi only bogey came at the par three 16th where he missed the green to the lef and hit a chip too strong.

On the second nine, Aaron started with a flourish. He birdied the firs hole after placing a great approach within 18 inches of the hole. On the par five second, he reached in two and got down with a pair of putts from 40 feet At the fifth, he cracked his approach two feet from the hole for another bird He bogied the eighth with only three putt green of the round.

Aaron's play, in contrast to his partners', was best described by Siffor on that par five second hole. After Tommy got his birdie to go four under an join the leaders on the scoreboards around the course, Sifford looked at Rodriguez and remarked unsmilingly: "We oughta let this guy play through."

Tommy spots 'em two, wins anyway

May 25, 1970

Unperturbable Tommy Aaron spotted a field of the world's finest golfers two strokes here yesterday and then horsewhipped them with his putter and coolness to win the Atlanta Golf Classic.

No, Aaron didn't step up on the first tee and announce he was giving everybody two shots. But he did inadvertently make a present of the important strokes just as he was pulling away from the field.

Fourteen under par and leading by two, Tommy teed off with a two-iron on the par four, 360-yard 14th hole. The effort came up much shorter than desired and Aaron and his caddy were discussing this when they reached the ball.

Because of so many bare spots on the Atlanta Country Club course, golfers were allowed to improve their lies in the fairway. It was commonplace for every player to do so on every hole the entire tournament.

Just as Aaron reached down and picked up his ball to improve it, he saw a white line in front of him which designated where the fairway started. He then suddenly realized he could not legally move his ball. He informed an official of the happening and was penalized two shots.

But all this took place away from his ecstatic gallery. Aaron then struck his approach to the green seven feet from the pin and sank for what everyone thought was a birdie. Unaware of what had taken place, Aaron's fans headed for the 15th overjoyed at what they thought was a three-shot lead.

The first inkling that something out of the ordinary had taken place came when George Knudson, Tommy's playing partner, stepped up to tee off first even though he had parred the 14th. Then the word began to spread concerning the penalty, and Aaron was placed at 13 under par on the scoreboards around the course. No one was sure of the details of the penalty at the time, but it came as a shock when Aaron's advantage over the field was cut from three to one shot.

Although Aaron later admitted he was a bit shaken by his error, his play didn't show it. He parred 15 and did the same at 16 even though he hit his tee shot in a trap. He blasted out six feet short and rammed the putt in.

After a par at 17, where a fine 30-foot putt refused to fall, Aaron teed off on the par five 18th, a good birdie hole. But his drive didn't carry quite far enough to the fairway, and he chose not to go for the green. He played safe and got his par.

While Tommy was playing 18, strong Tom Weiskopf picked up a birdie to pull into a tie for the lead.

As Aaron sat waiting in the scorer's tent, the talk was that Weiskopf had a good chance to get a birdie, but he put his tee shot into the water and ended up with a double bogey, two shots off the pace.

Aaron's winning round of 69, which would have been 67 without the event at 14, was a fine one.

No matter what the circumstances, the win was well deserved. Aaron played generally the best and steadiest golf of anyone in the tournament for the four days. He beat the field, the course and the penalty, and he did it in his home state before a host of his hometown fans.

Aaron's big one

April 11, 1973

Fans and writers do a lot of jawing about how this or that golfer might win a particular tournament. But the golfers themselves know they can't think about winning until they get into a position to do so.

Late Monday afternoon, Gainesville's Tommy Aaron got a chance to realize his personal dream. A chance to win golf's most cherished event, the Masters at Augusta National. He leaped upon that chance with both spiked feet, grabbed it, hugged it and protected it through the final pressurized holes like a man obsessed.

He knew his one-shot lead over J. C. Snead was precarious. But he wasn't about to do anything to lose it himself. If he was going to be overtaken, he was going to make Snead do the overtaking. You won't see any better example of coming through big in sports than Aaron showed Monday. And his gutty tenacity paid off with what will always be his biggest accomplishment in the game, a Masters championship.

Last Thursday night, after Aaron had surprised himself by shooting a 68 to take the first-round lead, he talked about his game, his career and the reasons he wanted a major victory so badly.

Aaron, myself and a friend Stan Davidson were relaxing over a steak at a place called the Cadaver Supper Club in Augusta and Aaron, as usual, talked in straight, matter-of-fact terms.

"I've been playing so poorly this year, that I'm surprised I shot 68 today,' Aaron remarked. "Certainly it would be great to win here, but you can never think about winning a tournament until it has reached a point where you have the opportunity to win."

Aaron emphasized that the money involved wasn't the main reason he wanted to win. "I've made lots of money playing golf, but that's not the big object now. So many people pull so hard for me, especially here, that I'd like to repay them in a major victory."

Pausing to accept wishes of good luck from a couple of passing fans he didn't even know, Aaron continued: "Also, it would be nice to shake that damned bridesmaid tag. I try not to let that bug me. If it were true about always finishing second, maybe I wouldn't mind. But it is unwarranted. Plenty of pro golfers have finished second many more times than me, but somehow I got stuck with it. I would like to end that once and for all."

The next two rounds, Aaron had some troubles with his swing at times. But he hung in there sinking enough knee-knocking little putts to give a man rickets. He refused time after time to give up on his game or himself. He had plenty of opportunities to do so, but he was too determined to remain in contention.

And remain in contention he did with rounds of 73 and 74 which were fair figures when you consider the event, the tough course and the way he hit the ball at times.

Then came his chance. It came on a sunny blustery day when he was striking the ball well, and he had made up a four-shot deficit with an excellent 32 on the front nine. When he rolled in another of those stomach-churning three-footers for a birdie at number 15, he had a two-shot lead. He knew then his opportunity was at hand. He knew then what he had to do over the final three holes.

He did it like the pro he is. He kept his game under control and made no mistakes. He figured he might need another birdie and tried to get one. Sometimes the toughest thing for a golfer to do is just make par when par is all he needs. Although he came agonizingly close at 18, Tommy didn't get another birdie and it turned out he didn't need one.

Aaron's exuberant fan support at Augusta (he was by far the big gallery favorite) almost proved detrimental. "People were urging me on so, I kept getting too charged up," he smiled. "I had to keep reminding myself to stay calm and not let them excite me."

Tommy Aaron says he wanted to thank his fans. But I want to thank Tommy Aaron. After more than 20 years in the writing game and at my age, I thought the day was past that I could be really thrilled by any sports happening. But Monday you thrilled me, Aaron. You had me shaking and gasping for breath. I don't mind admitting I temporarily blew my cool. It was worth it.

Now that Aaron has won the goldarned biggest golfball game they play, I would like to instruct my cohorts in the news media to take that word "bridesmaid," turn it sideways and ram it up your typewriters.

Tommy and Tommy show

June 26, 1977

I doubt that anyone keeps any records on such things, but it is a unique happening indeed when a town the size of Gainesville has two professional golfers good enough to compete on the PGA tour.

It is an even more rare happening that both Tommy Aaron and Tommy Valentine are next door neighbors on Wessell Road here.

The backgrounds of the two guys are strangely similar in a lot of ways. Both were fine quarterbacks when they played about 12 years apart at Gainesville High School. Both were all-around athletes who decided to concentrate on golf.

Aaron won two Southeastern Conference championships while at the University of Florida, and Valentine won the SEC when he was at Georgia. Both were selected collegiate All-Americans.

Before turning pro, Aaron played extensively on the amateur tour where he won some 15 tournaments and was runner-up in the U.S. Amateur.

The face of golf had changed considerably by the time Valentine came around and he chose to turn pro and play the mini-tour circuit where he won 10 events.

The two guys have been frequent golfing companions in practice sessions here, but it looks like they will be going against each other in a tournament for first time ever when the Greater Milwaukee Opens rolls around next week.

Aaron, who is on a break from the tour, says he plans to enter at Milwaukee. Valentine is playing this weekend in his very first PGA event at the Western Open. Since he survived the midway cut there, that means he won't be required to qualify at Milwaukee and has already earned a spot there.

The big difference between the two right now is their status as pros. The veteran Aaron, because he is among the top 50 all-time money winners, is an exempt player and is not required to qualify for regular tour events.

Valentine, on the other hand, is a rookie "rabbit." He would normally have to qualify by battling a host of others like him on Monday mornings prior to each tournament. But when a rabbit gets into an event and survives the cut, that means he is exempt from qualifying the following week. The rule now is that a rabbit must win at least $5,000 during the year or risk having his PGA player card pulled. The rabbit lives entirely by how well he plays.

While taking part in the same tournament, Aaron and Valentine can hardly afford to worry about each other because there is a large crowd of other golfers out there. But nobody likes to get beat by his next door neighbor.

When Aaron first joined the tour 18 years ago, he won money in the very

94

first event he entered and has been self-sustaining ever since. Valentine is also hoping to get off to a good money start.

When Valentine first turned pro, friend Hal McNeely of the Toccoa Casket Company considered sponsoring him.

The deal never came off, but, as a writer, I was hoping it would because I couldn't wait to type the words: "Tommy Valentine is the only pro on tour who takes six-foot divots." Come to think of it, maybe it's best I never got the chance.

One thing is for sure—following the pro golfing tour will now be twice as interesting.

Just a few cool ones

April 23, 1978

The dang do-gooders are at it again. I understand they've banned drinking on the golf course here. Ye gads, are there no limits to the infringements on individual rights?

Don't they realize the world is full of hackers who can't tolerate their bad play without a few cool beers to calm the nerves and steady the stroke for that three-foot putt that might salvage a double bogey?

Jack Nicklaus doesn't need to drink on the course. He knows how to play. But what about more than 90 per cent of the golfers on this planet who love to take their whacks but are unable to face the reality of high scores?

The rule is discriminatory. Nobody says you can't pop pills on the golf course. Thanks to the medical profession and other dope dealers, just about the whole world is on valium. Take away pills, and most of society couldn't operate.

I feel put upon. Three aspirin for a hangover is about my limit on the pill gig, but a few beers on the golf course seems almost a necessity. Especially after a drive out of bounds, one in the woods, two slash shots in a bunker and three putts. A hole like that would drive Gary Player to drink.

Dope pushers roam the streets, burglars and armed robbers abound, politicians are ripping off the universe, high prices and taxes are crippling the populace, a murder takes place every few minutes and the French are playing around with neutron bombs. And what does the establishment do? It says I can't drink beer on the golf course.

I mean, you know, I'm not gonna build a still out there. All I ask is a small cooler with a couple of frosty cans. I promise not to stagger, talk loud, attack my partner or throw empties on the ground. I just want a few to sip on.

Of course, the rule is only going to serve to drive us all underground. Thermos jugs will be brought into use, and some guys I know will probably fill up the hollow shafts of their clubs. Don't be surprised to see some long straws running to the bottom of golf bags.

I fully realize alcohol can cause evil, but so can money. You won't catch them banning cash from the golf course. Nothing would kill the game quicker.

I just might have to give up golf. The game would lose nothing because when I play, a real golfer can hardly bear to look.

But if I do continue to play, I'm warning those in authority now, you're gonna have to search me. You're gonna have to pat me down, frisk me and spread-eagle me. I mean, you're gonna have to do it on every hole.

When I tee up, rule or no rule, somewhere in the vicinity is going to be a bit of that soothing malt beverage that serves to loosen a bashful tongue, gladden a melancholy heart and ease the pain of ineptness.

Elephants, Ralston sweep state golf

May 12, 1981

Gainesville High's golf team and its number-one player, quiet and calm Mitch Ralston, won a pair of state Class AAA championships here yesterday, one the conventional way and the other the hard way, in a gruelling, pressurized 10-hole playoff.

On a raw, cold, windy and overcast day not conducive to good golf, the Red Elephant team grabbed its third Georgia title in the past four years, and Ralston became the first Gainesville player to win an individual crown since Tommy Aaron did it way back in 1955.

With the cold hampering concentration and the wind twisting shots around, the 96 young players from all over Georgia also faced the additional challenges of a Chattahoochee course which was stretched almost to its length limits, as well as some sadistic pin placements.

Scores reflected the conditions as Gainesville finished with a 319 total, five shots better than the 324 posted by defending state champion Thomson's 324. The other 14 teams finished even further behind.

Only eight players broke 80, and three of them were Red Elephants. Ralston's five over par 77 tied for low medal honors and most of his work was still ahead of him after that. GHS sophomores Joe Turner and Don Williams both shot 79 and Gainesville's number-four man, Marty Sykes, shot 84 but might have made the most important team contribution of the day.

The team battle was relatively close between GHS and Thomson even after Turner turned his first nine in one over par 37, Williams in 38 and Ralston in 39. It was evident that one of Gainesville's fourth, fifth or sixth golfers, either Sykes, Bryce Holcomb, Jr. or Bobby Grant was going to have to come in with something solid on their second nine after they turned at 45, 44 and 44.

Sykes did it with a fine 39 that, along with Ralston's 38 on the back, solidified the GHS lead.

After a brief bit of celebration for Gainesville's team title, Ralston had to go back out into the uncomfortable elements for an individual championship playoff against Cairo's Albert Rodenberry and Dalton's Bill McDonald who also shot 77s.

High school rules called for the trio to play three holes at 10, 17 and 18; and if a tie existed after that, it would be sudden death competition.

With a shivering gallery trudging along behind, the players were all a bit shaky on the first three holes, but an excellent second shot by Ralston at 18 kept him in a tie with Rodenberry as McDonald, a bespeckled freshman, was eliminated.

Off went Ralston and Rodenberry to number one to begin sudden death, and for the next six holes played just about as flawless a game of golf as could be performed by a pair of high schoolers.

Rodenberry, a husky, strong junior who is also a star lineman on the Cairo football team, used strong iron play to reel off par after par.

Steady Ralston, a smooth, slightly-built athlete who gave up baseball and football a couple of years ago to concentrate on golf, executed shot after shot and matched his rival.

The key for Ralston was probably the long, par three hole where he missed the green to the right and Rodenberry banged a great drive to the middle of the green.

Facing a difficult chip, Ralston chose to putt his ball over two mounds of terrain. His delicate shot was a beauty, ending up a foot from the hole and both got their pars.

With darkness gathering, things finally ended, sometime near 7 p.m., at the par four seventh. Ralston hit a perfect drive, but Rodenberry popped his up short, and then came up short of the green on his second.

Ralston got on in two, but some 70 feet from the pin. After Rodenberry chipped up and eventually two-putted for a bogey five, Ralston rapped his approach putt to within three feet and knocked in his par to end the long, cold day.

Ralston's steady play had reeled off eight straight pars to climax the senior's excellent career which saw him play on three state championship teams at Gainesville High.

Valentine hangs in there

June 8, 1981

Tommy Valentine didn't quite win the Atlanta Golf Classic yesterday, but he proved something to himself and a few thousand screaming supporters...he can handle the pressure game.

Losing to Tom Watson, regarded by many as the greatest player in the game today, is no disgrace. Valentine played eyeball-to-eyeball with Watson and could well have won the playoff. Actually, a sudden-death playoff is a rather flimsy way to decide a golf tournament. The fact is, a duffer with a spastic swing could very well beat the best player in the world on a given, single hole.

Be that as it may, Valentine had never before been in such a situation while Watson has been there many times. But this fact was not evident because Valentine matched Watson calm-for-calm.

Where Valentine truly displayed his mettle was well before the playoff came about, before the television cameras clicked on.

Through the first 15 holes of play, Valentine struggled and worked like a coolie laborer just to stay in the hunt. He hit only three of the first 15 fairways, didn't come close to a birdie, bogeyed the third hole by three-putting and bogeyed the 10th when he hit a tee shot that might still be screaming left through the wilderness had it not struck a tree.

But through this testing adversity, he kept saving gutsy pars, most all of them by making putts of six to eight feet. You know, the white-knuckle variety.

He was able to hang close because no one was making any hot runs toward taking a golf tournament that was just sitting there waiting to be taken. It is highly unusual for two players to shoot 71 and 72, as Watson and Valentine did, in the last round of a tournament and end up in a playoff for the title.

When Valentine got to the 16th hole, he was looking at a 15-foot birdie putt and was two shots back. He flat had to make that putt to have any chance at all of winning. He made it, to the tune of probably the loudest gallery cheer of the day.

At 18, a par five that can be had, all the cards were on the table. He had to make birdie four to tie. He did, by sinking another one of those danged five-footers that drive all golfers goofy.

Watson eventually won the playoff on the third extra hole when Valentine went boldly for the flagstick and flew his wedge shot into an almost impossible lie in the back of a bunker.

It was a very heady four days of golf for Valentine. Being a native son

nd all that good stuff, he was definitely the gallery favorite. Because he was
n All-American golfer at the University of Georgia back in 1970, the good ol'
oys in the crowd apparently considered him an extension of the Bulldogs'
ootball success this past season.

All around the course, loud guys were raising their beers on high and
shouting, "Go, you Dawg!" Non-natives might not believe it, but such com-
ments are considered highly complimentary in these parts.

Valentine and Calvin Peete, a straight-hitting dude who was also in the
running most of the way, turned out to be prophets. Prior to the final round,
both said they could win with a score of 68. Had either of them shot 68, they
would have won in a walk.

When the playoff was over, Valentine smiled, "I'm a tired little cowboy."

But things ain't all bad. Valentine's weariness will be eased somewhat
by that nice, $32,400 check he got for finishing second.

Working as caddie opened doors

August 8, 1982

When Gainesville native Sammie Griffin was a caddie at Chattahoochee
golf course here more than 20 years ago, he had no idea his interest in the
game would lead to his present occupation.

Griffin, who now lives in Bridgeport, Conn., works in purchasing and
distribution for Magco Golf Company, one of the largest golf equipment concerns in the world.

Home for a visit recently, Griffin recalled his early days as a caddie and
"basketball nut" here.

"When I was young, like a lot of black kids even today, all I was
interested in was playing basketball. Actually, I wasted a lot of time at
that game because it meant nothing so far as my future was concerned.
However, it did serve to keep me out of trouble at the time, so it wasn't a total
waste."

Griffin played basketball at Butler High School here, and after his
graduation in 1963, later played on the very first basketball team at
Gainesville Junior College.

"What I remember most as a caddie at Chattahoochee back about
1961 was the influence of men like Eph Matthews, Tom Paris, Perrin Reynolds
and the late Dr. John Scott who were the best amateur players here at that
time. We caddied for them and they did all they could to get us interested in
golf."

"Mr. Matthews would invite 10 or 12 of us kids to his house to practice chipping and putting."

"I also remember Tommy Valentine when he was a young player here, and I talked with Tommy Aaron not too long ago. I still closely follow their progress in golf."

"Also, my principal at Butler High, Ulysses Byas, encouraged us to devote more time to games like golf rather than limit ourselves to sports like basketball and football. Mr. Byas is still in education as a superintendent of schools at Long Island, N.Y."

Griffin's point is, he's committing himself to getting minority kids more interested in sports such as golf, tennis and other athletic endeavors rather than limiting themselves to the basic games such as basketball, football and baseball.

"There is nothing wrong with those major sports except the odds against any individual kid having a real future in them is very limited. Through the game of golf I got to meet a lot of quality people, and I still do, through my job and playing on an amateur circuit up around Bridgeport."

Griffin usually shoots in the mid-70's and has recently won several amateur events.

"My job and playing golf go hand-in-hand, and one enhances the other," says Griffin.

Griffin, who has coached on the high school level and works extensively with young people in recreation programs, was directed into his present occupation after he completed a speech class project on custom golf clubs and golf club construction.

Griffin, the son of Esther Patterson, the grandson of Mrs. Naomei Smith of Myrtle Street and the nephew of Miss Mattie Moon, a retired school teacher here, says he plans to keep in touch with youth programs here and hopes to encourage more local black youths toward golf.

Just before he left to return home to Bridgeport, Griffin was to play a round of golf here with LeRoy Harper, one of Gainesville's few black players.

"LeRoy is a pretty good player, but I can beat him," Sammie smiled. "I hope I can get LeRoy to help me lead more black kids into golf."

Pro golfer Chi Chi Rodriguez, Gainesville amateur Terry Maginnis, sportswriter Phil Jackson and Gainesville pro golfer Tommy Aaron all took part in a 1983 March of Dimes charity event played at the Big Canoe resort in the mountains of Pickens County.

Green thumbs help those green jackets

May 11, 1989

Any number of people from the Gainesville area have gone on to make it big in the world of sports, most of them as players or coaches.

Now you can add the name of Gainesville's Marsh Benson to the list, but in an entirely different area of athletic professionalism.

On June 1, Benson officially becomes the new superintendent of the famous Augusta National Golf Club course, home of the Masters Tournament.

Benson, at 33 years of age, has attained one of the most prestigious positions available in his profession, when you consider that the Augusta National course has for years been rated among the finest, most beautiful and most famous golfing layouts in the entire world.

101

Right now closing out a three-year tenure as superintendent of the Jennings Mill Country Club course in Athens, Benson maintains the quiet, pleasing personality he has always possessed.

"Getting the Augusta National position could be considered a dream," said Benson. "I'm certainly honored by the opportunity offered me, and I'm looking forward to the challenge."

Not that the Augusta National position has always been on Benson's mind, but it is the culmination of goals he set for himself when he was just 15 years old and a student at Gainesville High School where he was a member of the golf team.

"I decided then I wanted to try to make my living through golf, and I knew my game would never reach a professional level," said Benson.

"So, I sort of leaned toward golf course architecture and maintenance. I got some early help by working with Ron Sinnock who then was a very fine superintendent at Gainesville's Chattahoochee Golf Club."

Benson graduated from Gainesville High in 1973, went to Gainesville Junior College where he played on the golf team, and then went on to the University of Georgia for his degree in landscape architecture.

He worked in landscaping in Gainesville for a short time and then went on to take highly-regarded turf-grass studies at Penn State in 1981.

"I guess going through that program at Penn State sort of settled things so far as my future plans were concerned," said Benson. "Sinnock and many other successful golf course superintendents had taken the course, and completing it made up my mind."

Before moving to the Athens position, Benson was course superintendent at the Country Club of Florida in Boynton Beach, Fla.

Now fully involved in what has truly become a labor of love for him, Benson heads toward a golfing garden known as Augusta National, along with his wife, the former Becky Williams of Gainesville, and their two small children.

"Augusta National is a very special place," said Benson. "And I'm looking forward to working with the fine people there."

And so, another local boy makes good.

It's frenzy time again

March 20, 1990

It's started.

It happens every year about this time.

It's called April Frenzy and it's even worse than the March Madness of the NCAA basketball tournament.

It's the annual quest for tickets to the Masters Tournament to be played at the Augusta National Golf Club the first full week in April.

Oh, there are thousands of tickets to the Masters. But they are all taken. Sold out. They have been sold out for years.

There is a long, long waiting list. I believe some people have actually died of old age while sitting on that waiting list.

Since they started limiting the size of the crowd at the Masters some years ago, a ticket to one of the world's premier golfing events has become, without a doubt, the toughest ticket in sports.

Masters tickets, known as Series Badges, have been counterfeited, faked, stolen, scalped and blackmarketed.

Series Badges for the entire four days of the tournament have actually sold for thousands of dollars.

On the positive side, most Masters tickets are shared.

Most people who have the coveted tickets share them with family members, friends and sometimes even with desperate strangers.

But despite this kind and caring practice by many Masters ticket holders, known as Patrons, the quest for tickets seems to get a bit more wild each year.

The nice people who run the Masters, those dignified and gentlemanly wealthy guys who are members of the exclusive Augusta National Golf Club, attempt to be patient and fair about admittance to their international sporting event.

But they have had to get pretty tough about ticket policies.

Each year they send out a warning to their ticket holders.

In part, the warning says, "If you resell your badges through ticket brokers, travel agents, scalpers or other third parties, your name will be permanently removed from our Patrons list."

Hey, and they are serious about this. They have done this many times.

As a fortunate golf lover who has managed to get press credentials to the Masters for the past 36 years, I am often approached or called by people seeking tickets.

I have talked with hundreds of ticket seekers down through the years, despite my inability to be of any real aid.

But I do have a favorite Masters ticket story of all time, and I must repeat it once again.

Some years ago, a nice lady called me on the telephone and said, "I want to know how to get tickets to the Masters."

I told the lady there were no tickets available, and that they had been sold out for years.

But she was determined, and said, "Our neighbors go to the Masters every year. It's all they talk and brag about. I'm tired of listening to them. We have just got to have Masters tickets! I don't care if we have to sit in the end zone!"

Madge happy with fun career

October 2, 1990

Gainesville's Madge McDonald Zorn has won so many trophies and silverware in a long and successful amateur golfing career that she has given away more awards than she has kept.

In a competitive career that covered more than 30 years, Madge has repeated most of her championships many times over, and claims it was all just for the fun of it and that golf is a game to be enjoyed.

It would be impossible to list all of her championships because she has competed both in Georgia and Florida and does not even remember some of her wins.

Her top accomplishment was winning the Women's State Amateur championship three times and being named Georgia Woman Athlete of the Year in 1963.

It was coincidental that the Georgia Male Athlete of the Year in 1963 was Georgia Tech quarterback Billy Lothridge, also a Gainesvillian.

Madge's other wins include Georgia Senior Champion, 12 years; Northeast Georgia Women's Golf Association Champion, four times; Atlanta City Championship, seven times; Athens Country Club Champion, five times; and holder of the Chattahoochee golf course women's scoring record with a seven-under-par 65 set in 1974.

Madge recently donated 68 trophies to a local trophy shop because she has no room for them.

She stores 21 boxes of silver items won in various tournaments.

Over the years, Madge has often been urged to turn professional, but she has always chosen not to do so.

"I've played with professionals many times, but I've never turned pro. I've just never wanted to. Golf is a sport and fun for me. It's been wonderful just being an amateur," she said.

Although her serious competitive days are behind her, Madge still plays the game and says it's still fun.

Aaron grabs a milestone win

November 2, 1992

When Gainesville golfer Tommy Aaron recorded his first win on the Senior PGA Tour yesterday, it marked a successful career that now spans five decades.

Aaron sank a 20-foot birdie putt on his 18th and final hole to win the Kaanapali Classic in Hawaii to give him a one-shot edge over Dave Stockton.

Aaron's last golfing victory had come 19 years before in the 1973 Masters Tournament.

Aaron has now enjoyed success on every level of the golfing spectrum beginning with junior wins in the early 1950's and on up through the collegiate and amateur ranks, as a member of the U. S. Walker Cup team, the regular PGA Tour, two U. S. Ryder Cup teams and now on the Senior Tour.

At Kaanapali, Aaron's final round of seven-under-par 64 put him at 15-under-par 198 for the tournament and earned him the winner's purse of $75,000.

"It's great," Aaron said of his long victory drought. "I just wish it hadn't taken so long.

"That's the thing about golf. You can't blame your teammates. You work and struggle hard and you have your chances to win and you don't.

"You forget all about the close calls when you finally win again. I couldn't be happier. I played awfully well today."

Aaron joined the Senior PGA Tour in 1987, but until yesterday had yet to enter the winner's circle. Twice he came within one shot of victory earlier this year, only to lose in two playoffs to Mike Hill and George Archer.

Aaron's long golfing career, which blossomed again yesterday in the scenic splendor of Hawaii, got its start more than 40 years ago on the scruffy acres of Gainesville's old nine-hole municipal course that is now under the waters of Lake Lanier.

Aaron's late father, Charlie Aaron, was the pro at the old Gainesville course and taught his son the game that has brought Tommy fame and fortune.

CHAPTER 6

COACHES AND CAUSES

Many memorable coaches stalked the sidelines of local fields and arenas, and sports endeavors were often the center of various causes.

Well deserved award

January 28, 1962

Gainesville High Coach Graham Hixon—selected as Hall County's Young Man of the Year by Gainesville's Jaycees Friday night—is a many-sided fellow who belies the accepted image of a football coach.

His voice is quiet rather than gruff; he is a planner and technician on the field rather than a whip-cracking taskmaster; he talks of facts rather than alibis when recalling a defeat or looking toward a game to come; he does not possess nerves of steel, and his wit is dry and smiling rather than loud and boisterous.

His discipline methods with young athletes are designed to appeal to a boy's common sense rather than frighten him. As the Jaycee tribute said, Hixon is a scholar and teacher as well as a coach.

Hixon's refusal to be a "crying" coach has many times resulted in misunderstanding. When sportswriters call to check on Gainesville prospects for a coming season or a big game, Hixon truthfully gives his views and does not dwell heavily on weaknesses. Consequently, his teams are always among the favorites.

Left to right: Graham Hixon, Bobby Gruhn, and Georgia Tech head coach Bobby Dodd.

108

He is a pacer and a worrier before and during a game. Many times it takes hours for his nerves to calm down but even after a defeat his judgment is sound. He has never been known to blame anyone other than himself for a loss.

At every opportunity he gives credit to his assistants and players and many times is embarrassed when complimented.

In 1959, Gainesville had just whipped Avondale, 13-12, in an important game which eventually gave GHS the Region 4-AA title. After the contest, a fan rushed up and complimented Hixon on doing a fine job.

"Yes, I was really great tonight," the blond coach smiled nervously. "I sent three plays into the game all night. One lost yardage, the other was an incomplete pass and the quarterback refused to run the third one."

The Jaycees could not possibly have picked a more worthy recipient of their award. Graham Hixon is the type man who can do only good for our youngsters.

About Little League

May 12, 1963

The world of sports often is filled with controversy but nothing in the professional or college ranks even comes close to Little League baseball where dispute is concerned.

Gainesville's National Little League had hardly heard the crack of the first bat before letters to newspapers, phone calls and sidewalk gripes were being aired. As usual the parents do most of the mouthwork. The boys themselves would just like to play a little baseball.

One of the most recent complaints concerns the condition of the City Park field used by the National Minor League and the fact that many minor leaguers don't get to play enough. There is nothing wrong with a little griping except that most complainers merely yell about problems but never have any suggestions as to possible solutions.

Concerning the condition of the minor league field, the Park and Recreation Department tried to remedy the "red dirt bank" problem early this season by planting grass. But the hoards of youngsters who continually play in the area stomped it all away. As the old saying goes, it's impossible to grow grass on a race track.

Many kids in the minors don't get to play often because there are only enough managers for a certain amount of teams and most of these teams have more than 20 boys on them.

If some of the parents complaining about this would volunteer their services as managers, there would be more teams and boys would get to play more often. Minor leaguers do not have full uniforms because the sponsoring Gainesville Touchdown Club does not have the funds to completely equip both the majors and minors.

If every father of a Little Leaguer would just pay $20 annually and join the Touchdown Club, there would be enough money to provide uniforms for all. If you care to help in this area, just send your membership check to Gainesville Touchdown Club, Box 120.

Of course, there is one vast solution to the entire problem of Little League—just abandon the entire program.

I believe that the good points of Little League override the bad ones, but if a child's athletic program is going to be taken over completely by adults and the boys themselves are merely going to be checkers on a checkerboard, then it's not worth it.

Many parents use Little League as a free babysitter service during the summer. Others are interested only in their boy and take no interest whatsoever in the overall program. I have great respect for the men who volunteer as managers, but many times they lose sight of the fact that they are working with small, uncoordinated boys and not major leaguers.

It really might not be so bad going back to unorganized, sandlot ball. Just think, boys, you get to choose up for teams among yourselves and you wouldn't have to put up with the "point-bid" system devised and arrived at by adults. You would make your own rules and there would be no adult umpires to argue over rule books with adult managers. You could settle your own disputes and, by golly, you might get a chance to think for yourself for a change!

There are more vacant lots and pastures than expensive Little League fields. Anything will serve as a base and new balls and bats will not be mandatory. There would be no mimeographed schedule to follow. You would play when you felt like it, and you wouldn't be in danger of getting chewed out if you failed to show up because you just didn't want to play on any given day.

The major leagues and other areas of the business world are filled with successful men who had no experience with Little League baseball. It is not absolutely necessary, and it certainly isn't a life and death situation. But some adults take it too seriously when it is merely supposed to be "fun and games" for the kids.

I think supervised recreation is best, but you can easily over-supervise and over-emphasize.

Little League would be as good for our youngsters if it were left to them. As it is, they are becoming little robots in bright caps who can hardly play a simple game of baseball without being smothered by adults who often act more childish than the children themselves.

If you want to keep Little League, try to help solve the problems and enjoy the games. A loss isn't death and a win isn't the world championship.

The quiet man
March 12, 1965

Look on the benches at most high school basketball tournaments today and you will see nervous, intense young men in button-down collars and fashionable blazers. While constantly talking and sometimes gesturing wildly, they may, at times, consult with assistants who carry shot charts and other technical data recorded during the course of a game.

These are the modern-day coaches. They are students of basketball. They are excitable. They sometimes berate officials. They sometimes berate their players. They are dedicated and hard working. They are the new breed. Color them okay guys, because most of them are.

But the next time you have a chance, look on the end of the bench occupied by the girls basketball team of Forsyth County High School of Cumming, Ga. You won't see a crewcut, or a blazer, or any nervousness or any of the trappings of the spaceage world. You will just see one of the most successful basketball coaches and quietest gentleman you will ever have the pleasure to know.

He is D. B. Carroll. Color him a winner for more than 25 years of coaching. His hair is average length and average gray. His ties and suits are dark and conservative. His collars turn up their noses at buttons. He talks quietly to his players only during timeouts. He talks to officials only when he thinks it necessary. And even when he talks, he is a man of few words.

At Georgia Tech's gleaming, gold and white Alexander Memorial Coliseum yesterday morning, Coach Carroll spoke quietly just before his girls went out and beat Calhoun in double overtime to lead off the female division of the State Class AA tournament.

The conversation lasted only about five minutes, but the reporter talking with Coach Carroll managed to learn a few general and unchronicled facts about him. In his years of coaching high school teams at Canton, Jasper and Cumming, he has kept no actual count of the large number of teams he has taken to state tournaments. He remembers that the first one to play in state competition went to Athens when Woodruff Hall was considered the basketball palace of the South.

He admits that teenagers have changed over the years, but he does not agree with the talk that our young folks are going to the dogs. "There were some bad characters when I was a teenager and there are some now. But there are more good youngsters than bad," he said as he looked around at a large crowd of high school students gathered to watch the tournament games. "I'm not worried about them. The automobile now seems real important to them and they have a lot more to do and more places to go but they are better than a lot of people seem to think."

Coach Carroll is by nature a quiet man. He is not impressed with his long and successful career. When congratulated on winning the 4-AA championship and reaching the state, he smiled, gazed around the spacious coliseum and replied: "I'm just proud we got this far, and I'm hoping we can go on a little further." With a wave of his hand, he moved his tall frame across the hardwood toward his bench.

As I watched him amble away, I thought about what Coach Clarence Dennard of Chestatee once told me. Dennard, one of the young, bright coaches, stated: "D. B. Carroll has already forgotten more basketball than most of us will ever learn."

I recall the night when one of his teams won one of his last state championships.

As the game ended, players and fans were going berserk in celebration at midcourt.

I looked for Coach Carroll, and there he was, gathering up his practice basketballs and calmly putting them away in a canvas bag, as if it were merely the end of another practice session.

Coach Carroll may not win himself another state championship this time around. But even if he doesn't, those button-down collars will still have to look up to him.

We lose a showman

May 9, 1965

When the current school term ends, Lanierland stands to lose one of the most flamboyant and likable fellows in the high school football coaching profession.

Ken Paxton is his name and offense is his game. Paxton is leaving his position as head football and track coach at South Hall High School. If he departs completely from the area sports scene, it will be a bit like removing the red, yellow and green colors from the crayon box. And without them, things could get pretty dull around the ol' coloring book.

In three years at South Hall, Paxton has made memorable contribuions in the fields of public relations, athletic attendance, participation, competitive spirit and proper mental attitudes among athletes. All his contributions have not been intangible. Since he took over the football reins at the home of the Knights, paid attendance at games is six times more than it was the season he arrived.

It took no profound thinking on Paxton's part to boost his programs. He just used common sense in (1) making sure all news media remained familiar with him, his teams, his athletes and his schedules; (2) moving his home football games to Saturday night to beat the Friday night conflict with other schools in the area; (3) installing a wide-open pro style offense to please the crowds as well as win football games; (4) dressing his players in stylish uniforms and traveling clothes and creating an atmosphere of real "class" and self-confidence among his athletes as well as members of the student body and faculty.

Paxton pulled the football team from last in the region in 1962 to a sub-region championship in 1963 and a second-place in the sub-region last season. In track, his flying Knights are undefeated in dual meet competition over the past three seasons. He brought his track program along so well that he actually drew paying customers to his meets. This has seldom been done at any school in this part of the state.

Of course, you can't mention Ken Paxton without talking about a young man named Jerry Paul who may well be the finest athlete ever to come out of his area. Paul has been the sparkplug of Paxton-coached teams for three years.

Paul was Georgia Prep Back of the Year in Class AA last season and the state 100 and 220 yard dash champion. A fantastic ball-carrier, Paul accounted for his share of the 93 touchdowns Paxtons' Knights scored in three seasons. Needless to say, Paul contributed a great deal to the attendance record.

Paxton's athletic background is filled with big names in the sports world. A native of Louisville, Ky., he was a childhood playmate of Pee Wee Reese of major league baseball fame.

While attending Purdue University and taking part in football and track, Paxton coached a junior high team at Lafayette, Ind. One of his young halfback standouts was a fellow named Bob Friend who has been an outstanding pitcher for the Pittsburgh Pirates for a number of seasons.

For 24 years Paxton held the Kentucky high school record of 2:01 in the 880 yard run. He set the mark in 1934 and for three straight seasons he was the state 880 and 440 champion.

One of Paxton's most fond sports memories is of 1933 when he competed in the National Intercollegiate and Interscholastic track meet held at Soldier's Field in conjunction with the World's Fair in Chicago.

113

One of the many nervous state high school track champions, Paxton had a locker next to that of the great Kansas miler, Glenn Cunningham. Paxton warmed up with Cunningham prior to the events that night. While Paxton was placing fourth in the national high school 880, Cunningham set a new mile record and Jesse Owens, just a high schooler himself, ran a 9.4 hundred yard dash.

A bachelor, an extremely immaculate dresser and a fast-talking fellow who likes new cars, Paxton has been called a showboat and a publicity hound by those who miss the point of his personality. He may be all of these, but it has paid off and brought South Hall to the front as a "name" school in these parts.

We hate to see Paxton go. We will miss the laughing conversations and his flare for the colorful.

Right now, Paxton doesn't know his destination. But wherever he lands a coaching position, the fans will know immediately that Paxton and his athletes are there and wanting to be heard and seen.

We wish him the best of luck and another Jerry Paul.

Ball sounds the call

July 27, 1966

A personable fellow named Bubba Ball is here and his mere presence should mean a great deal to the sport of basketball in the Lanierland area.

Ball is the athletic director and head coach at the new Gainesville Junior College and is wasting no time getting his programs underway even though construction at the Oakwood school site is still going on.

"We start basketball practice September 22 at the South Hall High School gym and we want players. We don't want to discourage any student from trying out. Some of the best players in junior college ranks are students who just showed up for practice as unknowns," says Ball.

Gainesville College will give no scholarships and there is no recruiting, as such. Coach Ball says the school plans to play a full junior college basketball and baseball schedule.

A 44-year-old native of Alabama, Ball comes here from Baker High of Columbus where he coached 15 years and earned the reputation as one of the finest teachers of basketball in the state.

When asked about his record at Baker, Ball flashed a big grin and recalled: "We won two state championships, blew two more and gave four away," he laughed.

114

Even though he has gained fame through basketball, most of Ball's playing career was dedicated to baseball. He spent eight years as a professional in the Cardinal and Pirate organizations.

As a player, he made stops at Columbus, Miami, Lake Charles, San Antonio and DeLand. "I never hit under .300 anywhere," he points out. "But they could never find a place for my glove. I tried numerous positions." Although he missed five years of pro ball while in the U.S. Navy during World War II, Ball got managerial years in Alabama with Opelika, Andalusia and Headland.

However, his basketball background was not neglected since he played for three years in the old Southern Professional Basketball League.

One of the programs Ball has in mind is a summer basketball clinic for young players. "If we can make a success of training programs of this type, we can develop basketball in this area and won't have to go outside for playing prospects."

Ball is well aware that this is mainly football country, but he doesn't mind that because he is a gridiron fan also. His aim is to bring basketball up to an interest level with football. "Training players when they are young will help high schools and junior colleges in this area," he believes.

There is not yet a nickname nor school colors for Gainesville Junior College, but Bubba Ball is on the job, and he brings with him an air of confidence and exciting times to come.

Are you a basketball player interested in learning the game from one of the best? Apply Gainesville Junior College, Oakwood, Ga.

Ivey merely wanted lumber, ended up coaching kids

April 25, 1967

One day in 1957, Ted Ivey started out to acquire a bit of scrap lumber and ended up with a coaching career.

If you are familiar with the Gainesville sports scene, you know Ted Ivey. He's that lean, friendly guy in the railroad cap and overalls who has had something or another to do with sports in these parts for more than 20 years.

An employee of the Gainesville Midland and Seaboard Railroads for 19 years, Ted is now mainly a spectator at most ballgames. But up until this year, he has either played in, promoted or coached various athletic events.

115

When his working hours were changed just recently, it meant he would have to end coaching and managing teams in the Gainesville National Little League system. The way he got started in this pastime is a story in itself.

It seems Ted was promoting one of his six amateur basketball tournaments which were called the Candler Invitational and held at Candler Elementary School gym. Ted needed some scrap lumber for repairs at the aged gym so he went to see Bryan Springle who was in the lumber business in the area.

When Ted asked about the price of the lumber, Springle—who was at that time coaching a minor league team and was destined to become commissioner of the National Little League—had a trade in mind. He told Ivey: "I'll give you the lumber if you'll come out and help us work with the kids."

Ivey agreed and—as most folks do who get closely involved with schoolboy athletic programs—he became "hooked." For the next 10 years he worked in Little League, spent five of those years coaching midget football and three of them in the Pony League program.

Ivey's involvement in Little League and promotion were not his first connections with sports. Starting in the 1940's he was an outstanding amateur basketball player with such teams as the McEver Packers of Talmo and Chicopee.

He played in the days when industrial league basketball was highly popular in these parts. Ted and those of his breed played because they loved it. In one stretch of 15 days, he recalls playing in 14 basketball games.

His personal baseball experience consisted only of what he calls "pasture league" play. A native of the Talmo area, he pitched and caught in rural competition against teams from communities such as Walnut and Plainview in Jackson County.

The 45-year-old railroader currently spends time when he can at Gainesville High baseball games because a lad named David Chester is the ace pitcher for the Red Elephants even though he is only a sophomore. David is Ivey's stepson and at least partially a product of Ted's coaching. Ted's wife, Colleene, is also an avid sports fan, follows the games closely and has been active in auxiliary work in Little League and Pony League.

Ivey still maintains a close connection with the schoolboy athletic programs and helps out where he can. But mostly he just enjoys watching the young athletes perform as they come up through a chain of development which he has been an important part of for so many seasons.

You don't know Ted Ivey? Just look for the guy in the railroad hat with his hands tucked in the pockets or stuffed in the bib of a pair of overalls. If he's watching a ballgame, that's Ted Ivey.

Fond memory for successful coach

August 8, 1967

Gainesville's Drane Watson is a man with many fond sports memories. But probably his fondest was emphasized here recently when the Gainesville High School football team of 1947 held its 20th anniversary reunion.

Watson, now vice president and sales manager for Paris-Dunlap Hardware Company here, coached that amazing team which has to rank as one of the most outstanding in modern Red Elephant history.

The accomplishments of that team are a matter of record. It played 13 games, had 10 victories, two ties and a single loss. The lone defeat didn't come until the state championship encounter with a massive Valdosta aggregation.

Probably the most impressive statistic concerned the first 12 game when the Elephants rolled up 275 points while allowing the opposition only 12. A fine Griffin team led by Pete Ferris scored six of those points in a 6-6 tie and traditional rival Athens got the other six as GHS took a 46-6 victory.

Watson's Elephants opened with a 48-0 win over Winder, nipped Elberton 12-0, slew Waycross 44-0, tied 6-6 with Griffin, battled to a 0-0 tie with a powerful Decatur team, topped Marietta 20-0, whipped Russell 32-0, knocked off North Fulton 19-0, stung LaGrange 6-0, toppled Spalding 26-0 and routed Athens 46-6 to complete a regular season of nine wins and two ties.

In the North Georgia Football Association playoff, GHS took the measure of a fine Rockmart team, 13-0. Now NGFA champs and NGIC co-champs with Decatur, the Elephants traveled to Albany to collide with Valdosta for the state title.

Valdosta, led by quarterback Billy Grant and halfback Sonny Stephenson, finally wore the Elephants down with a superior weight advantage and took at 24-12 win.

Watson will be the first to admit he was blessed with a number of fine athletes that season, but he had an unusually lightweight team for such an impressive record.

Co-captain George Dobbs was Lineman of the Year in Georgia that season and he played tackle at 175 pounds. Co-captain Jimmy Henson would have to lie a bit to reach 150, but he played both offense and defense.

Jack Roberts, still considered by some as the finest all-around high school athlete ever to perform in Georgia, tipped the scales at about 150 but could do more than everything.

Heroes were numerous that year and people close to that team will never forget it.

117

Coach Watson enjoyed many good days. He tutored outstanding track and basketball teams. In 1949 Watson's baseball squad picked up the state crown by beating Albany, Canton and Fulton right here at City Park.

His fellow coaches named him president of their state association and he coached the North team in the annual high school all-star football contest.

He received the highest honor that can be bestowed on a state high school figure when he was elected to the Georgia Prep Sports Hall of Fame.

Yes, Drane Watson can recall many accomplishments as a coach and teacher. But his biggest smile beams when you mention that football team of 1947.

Builder from Bessemer

October 18, 1967

Coach E. G. Taylor has a background for building a successful high school football program and his system is already showing progress in his first season at the home of the North Hall Trojans.

With three games yet to play, Coach Taylor's surprising charges have won four games, which is more than any other North Hall team ever won in a decade of competition. This might not sound like an impressive record to the casual observer, but you must remember that there are only 16 players on the entire varsity.

Five years ago Taylor got his first head coaching job at Villa Rica and was greeted by a varsity consisting of just 16 players. When he left there to accept the North Hall position this season, Villa Rica had 65 boys out for the varsity and a B-team program underway.

Despite his small team at North Hall, Coach Taylor did not hesitate to start a B-team which currently consists of 11 players.

"Our big job is building and maintaining interest in football," says Taylor. "In order to do that you've got to win, and we hope there are some winning seasons in the future. We have eight sophomores on our starting team and will lose only four players to graduation."

North Hall has been out of region competition for a couple of seasons but Taylor plans to put the Trojans back into contention in 1968. "Playing in a region will help the interest in the team so we will return next fall," says Taylor.

Born in Talladega, Ala, and a star high school guard at Bessemer, the 35-year-old Taylor has high praise for his North Hall players. "In all my coaching career, I can't remember ever having a group with more enthusiasm. They

118

vant to play and win and are willing to pay the price of working hard. I'm very pleased with them. They are a fine group of boys."

Coach Taylor speaks from experience when he talks of the price a player must pay because he played himself for four years at Bessemer, one season as a freshman after getting a scholarship to the University of Florida, two years of service football with the U.S. Army and then three more at Jacksonville State in Jacksonville, Ala.

It was at Jacksonville State that he met his wife, the former Myra Richey of Geraldine, Ala. The couple now resides on Mt Vernon Road, in Murrayville with their two sons, Richie, 8, and Shane, 5, who are students at Lanier School.

Taylor went immediately into coaching after graduation in 1960. He started as an assistant at Buchanan, was line coach for two years at Banks High in Birmingham and then moved to to Villa Rica as head coach.

Working with a squad of only 16 players poses many problems. If a couple of key players happen to be absent for some reason, the drills are "just about wrecked," says Taylor. "We have to use a half-line when we scrimmage and have to work the right side against the left in turn. But we expect more players next season because interest in the program is already growing."

Coach Taylor has a chance to post the very first winning season in North Hall history. But even if he doesn't, he already has laid a fine foundation for a solid football program and a bright athletic future.

Dean of Hall coaches

May 12, 1968

W. H. (Dub) Jones is leaving his position as head basketball coach at East Hall High School, and his departure means the county is losing its "dean" of coaches.

Right now, Jones is the sole surviving coach who was on hand at any of Hall County's three high schools when they opened their doors 11 years ago. He has been at the head of every East Hall Viking boys basketball team there ever was and things won't be the same around "Valhalla" (Viking heaven) when he is gone.

During his prep coaching career, which included some time at old Riverbend High, Jones has a lifetime won-loss record of 209-184 and many of his teams are memorable ones. Especially the 1958 "Wonderous Wizards of White Sulphur" who shocked the prep basketball scene by winning the Region 7-AA championship and going all the way to the state semi-finals in East

119

Hall's first year of existence. One of Dub's fine Riverbend teams also earned a state berth.

The blond and personable Jones has coached 23 boys who went on to college and 16 of them made their college teams. Eleven of his pupils have become coaches and teachers. One of them, Eddie Waldrep, will probably succeed him at East Hall.

It seems that Dub has been associated with sports even back to his childhood days when he was runner-up in a district marble tournament at 11 years of age. He was captain of his high school basketball team at Airline.

He entered the U.S. naval air corps in 1943, rose to the rank of first class petty officer at the age of 18 and received a commendation from the Secretary of the Navy. He was even associated with celebrities while in the service. He played on a baseball team with the great Ted Williams and flew with entertainers Arthur Godfrey and Caesar Romero who were in his air wing.

After his discharge, he held jobs at New Holland and Chicopee mills, played baseball and basketball with New Holland and basketball with Chicopee. He attended the University of Georgia nights and part-time from 1949 until 1951 and graduated from Piedmont College in 1954.

He was a teacher, coach and school bus driver at Lula for one year before moving on to Riverbend and eventually East Hall. He received his masters degree from Peabody College in 1965.

During his early years in coaching at East Hall, Jones was a fiery fellow on the sidelines. Now 43 years old, he has mellowed some in recent seasons but, like any successful coach, he never reached the point that losing was easy to accept.

Along with coaching, Dub has always had a liking for politics and always keeps himself informed on local, state and national governmental doings. He was an unsuccessful candidate for the state legislature in 1964 and some say his future possibly lies in the political field.

Jones is married to the former Louise Hopkins, and they live with their five children on a 12-acre tract of land near Springway Church just off the Cornelia Highway.

Basketball will continue on at East Hall, even without Dub Jones. But he will always be remembered as the guy who got the Vikings off to a winning start and contributed so much to the sport in our area.

Deavers and Dude were first

December 20, 1968

It was reported recently that when Bobby Gruhn and Dale Vezey were named coach and lineman of the year in Georgia, it marked the first time in the history of Gainesville High School that both a coach and a player were so recognized.

'Taint so.

This high honor belongs to Coach Clayton Deavers and end Billy Joe (Dude) Thompson who won the top awards in Class A back in 1952.

Coach Deavers, not long out of the University of Georgia where he played fullback and guard, had a talented group of small but fast and flashy Red Elephants.

The team was not highly ranked before the season started, but it went on to accomplish some of the most memorable feats in the rich history of Gainesville High football. Swift fullback Harry Wing, stumpy quarterback Bud Cummings, and hard-running halfbacks Billy Vardeman and Charles Healan were the chief offensive threats along with the pass-catching and running ability of Thompson.

Rugged Bobby Howard, Bert Doss and Jim Patterson were defensive standouts in the line.

Competing in Region 4-A, the Elephants of '52 were not highly regarded prior to the season, but they soon gained statewide notice. They won their first eight games in a row, dropped two, went on to the region championship and weren't stopped until the North Georgia playoffs.

One week after halting Rockmart's 14-game winning streak, 21-0, the Elephants then pulled off the biggest victory in Georgia prep circles that year.

Decatur was considered the king of high school football in our state at that time. The Bulldogs rolled into City Park on Oct. 12 riding a 29-game winning string. With Thompson making an unforgettable touchdown run on an end-around, Gainesville stunned Decatur, 12-0, in one of the greatest wins ever for a GHS team.

Besides Decatur and Rockmart, GHS also downed West Fulton, Monroe, Griffin, Spalding, Athens and Ellijay in order before losing to LaGrange, 14-0, and Elberton, 13-7.

In another memorable game which still has many long-time Gainesville fans talking, the Elephants defeated Spalding again, this time 19-12 for the 4-A West title at Grady Stadium in Atlanta. The victory came on next to the last play of the game when Cummings—faced with a fourth and five situation at his own 35—passed to Thompson who ran by a few folks for an electrifying, 65-yard touchdown.

121

GHS then enjoyed a measure of revenge by beating Elberton, 7-0, fo
the region championship. A state title dream ended when Newnan won th
North Georgia title, 12-7.

Those state honors for Deavers and Thompson followed. Thompson
after a hitch in the Navy, played linebacker for Georgia's 1959 Southeastern
Conference and Orange Bowl champions.

Deavers is now in the insurance business here and Thompson make
his living in the construction game. But no matter how successful they migh
be, they will always be better known locally with their football accomplish
ments.

Most with the least

August 10, 1975

A nice guy has departed the local high school coaching ranks, but he'
still with us in another capacity which will keep him in close contact with
young people, and this is good.

Homer Cuddy is no longer football coach of the East Hall Vikings, bu
he remains an assistant principal at the school where for the past seven year
he has turned in a dedicated football effort.

Anyone who takes over the football job at East Hall starts out at a dis
advantage, because it is no secret that East Hall is a basketball school. It ha
a rich tradition for turning out winning basketball teams and individuals wh
have gone on to play on the college level, and then into the coaching profession

Homer Cuddy actually worked wonders with the football program at th
home of the Vikings. Most of the time with a squad of less than 30 players
Cuddy's teams were always competitive in one of the toughest Class A region
around.

He didn't have any championship teams, but his small, physically
rugged players pestered the contenders and no one ever took them lightly. H
had consecutive 8-2 and 7-3 seasons with player material that wasn't sup
posed to even come close to stacking up with the opposition.

But Cuddy worked hard and instilled some of his determination into hi
players, who time and again performed better than they were physically capa
ble. It was not unusual for Cuddy to have players at 120 and 130 pounds doing
good jobs at key positions.

He always gave his athletes all the credit, but it was no secret among
area coaches that Cuddy probably did the finest coaching job of them all, con
sidering what he had to work with.

122

Because of a lack of depth, Cuddy's small nucleus of good players had to perform a variety of duties and play full time. Consequently, he was almost always hampered by injury problems.

But first and foremost in Cuddy's mind, was the safety of the young men who played for him. There were times when his better players were hampered by hurts, but probably could have played. But Cuddy always believed that no game was worth the health of a youngster, and he would take a licking rather than take a risk.

I remember once Cuddy lost a game because he had a reserve player in a position he couldn't handle. "The kid just couldn't get the job done," Cuddy said after the game "But he gave it all he had, and that's all any of us can ask of a player."

I hate to see Homer Cuddy leaving the coaching ranks. But I'm glad he will still be working with the youngsters of East Hall, because he is a man who genuinely cares.

Two for 100

October 2, 1975

Gainesville High School coaches Bobby Gruhn and Chuck McDonald, who just last weekend reached the milestone of 100 victories as football tutors at the home of the Red Elephants, are actually an unlikely pair.

The fact that they have been together for 13 years here, and managed such an enviable record, is a tribute to their dedication and pure love for their demanding profession. The fact is they are almost complete opposites, except for being able to agree on just how winning football should be played.

Gruhn, the head coach and mainly a teacher of interior line play, is a big guy who, at times, is vocal and gruff on the practice field and during a game. He cajoles, prods and demands. He can be impatient to the point of exasperation. Away from the playing field, he appears rather bashful, especially when confronted with praise.

McDonald, the chief assistant and offensive specialist, is a small, studious type fellow. An excellent classroom teacher, McDonald even maintains an academic demeanor while coaching. He is a meticulous student of the game, always intent on the smallest details of just how a backfield should execute a play. Football practice to McDonald is a laboratory class preparatory to a final exam.

Gruhn likes to kid about his personal coaching philosophy by saying with a smile: "You've got to treat dumb linemen like dumb linemen. I know, I was a dumb lineman myself."

Ask McDonald a question about how his backs are doing, and it's like feeding a card into a computer. He reels off a bunch of statistics. You get everything but the flashing lights.

Gruhn has actually been at GHS 21 years. For his first eight seasons, he was line coach under Graham Hixon. When Hixon left to accept the coaching position at Woodward Academy in College Park, a spot he still holds, Gruhn took over the top post.

Herein lies the irony of the success of the Gruhn-McDonald combination.

The first three years they directed the Elephants, their teams had consecutive records of 3-7, 3-7 and 3-7. The reason for this was Gainesville High was forced, by a vote of the city board of education, to compete in Class AAA, even though GHS was only a Class AA school. Gainesville teams were seldom embarrassed in those days, they were simply out-manned by schools which many times had three times the student enrollment of Gainesville.

When you have three straight losing seasons, especially in a town with a rich football tradition, the wolves begin to howl. It happened here. Many fans blamed the lack of wins on coaching and campaigned for a change.

Luckily, Gruhn and McDonald weathered the storm and Gainesville was allowed to return to Class AA, where it should have been all the time, in 1966.

That year, the Elephants won the Region 8-AA championship, got to the North Georgia playoffs and had a 10-2 record. It was the beginning of a string of big seasons as the Elephants won the region title eight of the next nine years, numerous sectional titles, three North Georgia crowns and got to the state finals three times.

From 1966 through 1972, GHS won seven straight region championships without losing a single region game, a record unequaled by any other school in Georgia.

The credentials of Gruhn and McDonald right now stand at 100 wins, 45 defeats and four ties. Since 1966 when GHS returned to its rightful classification, the record is 91 wins, 24 losses and four ties.

That ain't bad for a "dumb" lineman and a quiet science teacher who almost weren't given a fair chance to show what they could do with a bunch of high school football players.

Maxie memory

December 12, 1978

After 19 years at Banks County High School in Homer, good ol' Coach Maxie Skinner is taking over as recreation director for Habersham County.

Actually, Maxie isn't "moving" anywhere because he has lived in Demorest all these years, right in the town where he was an All-American basketball player some 22 years ago.

While playing for little Piedmont College, Skinner was the fourth leading collegiate scorer in the nation when he averaged 32.8 points a game and scored more than 2,000 points in his college career which closed in 1956.

What a deadly gunner Maxie was. I remember watching him play college basketball, but what I remember most is years after his collegiate career was over, he played in what were called "amateur" basketball tournaments at places such as Bethlehem and Candler.

Those get-up tournaments, long since outlawed by the NCAA, brought together a conglomeration of basketball players from colleges, high schools, recreation leagues and some guys right off the street and out of pool rooms.

There were no entry rules, just get up a team, pay an entrance fee and play. It was not unusual to see a team of guys nearing 40 years of age taking on a college team from Clemson, Georgia or Oglethorpe playing under the name of Joe's Hamburger Palace or Godfrey's Service Station.

The tournaments were interesting, but they died when the NCAA banned active college players. It seems the word got out that Joe's Hamburger Joint and Godfrey's Service Station were known to slip a few bucks to the players in return for their performances.

Anyway, getting back to Skinner, even when his hair was turning grayish and his midsection preceded him across the center line, he could still shoot that basketball. Nobody played any defense, so it was a shooter's game. I would expect to this very day that Skinner can still thread that ol' onion sack.

After graduating from Piedmont in 1956, Skinner coached at old Toccoa High School, spent a couple of years in the Army and joined the coaching staff at Banks County in 1959.

Enticed by a $750 coaching supplement, Skinner coached varsity football, both varsity basketball teams, boys and girls B-teams, boys and girls eighth grade teams and baseball.

During his career at Banks County, Skinner took 14 boys and girls teams to state tournaments and was named coach of the year three times.

When Maxie started coaching at Banks County High, there were three athletic trophies in the building, and now there are more than 100.

One of the biggest and most unusual wins for Skinner came a couple of seasons ago in a sub-region basketball tournament. Rabun County was heavily favored over Banks. So Skinner, belying his personal reputation as a gunner, had his team hold the ball the entire game and finally got a 3-2 win.

I just want to wish Maxie well in his new endeavor in Habersham County.

But here's a word of warning to the youngsters Maxie will now be working with. Don't play h-o-r-s-e with Skinner, because that shooting touch is more than likely still with him.

Sweet music got Post 7 to nationals

August 29, 1979

Coach Don Brewer is a lover of bluegrass music. Put him in a room with a recording by Bill Munroe and the Foggy Mountain Boys, and Brewer's in heaven.

But not even the stirring strains of "Orange Blossom Special" are as pleasing to Brewer as the tune just thumped out by his Gainesville Post 7 American Legion baseball team.

Now, the ping of an aluminum bat sounds nothing like a banjo, a fiddle or even a five-string mandolin, but Brewer would prefer that sound when his team plays for a national championship in Greenville, Miss., this week.

A Georgia championship and a Southeastern Regional championship have already been won by Brewer's young baseball band, and the reward is an appearance in the biggest hoedown of all, the American Legion World Series.

Whether you're making good music or playing good baseball, there has to be a certain chemistry, and Brewer's collection of youngsters from the foothills of the Blue Ridge Mountains has struck the right note.

"I know this sounds like a typical coach's quote," said Brewer, "but it's true. We got exactly the contributions we needed from each of our players at different times. Somebody either threw the right pitch, made the right defensive play or got the big hit at just the right time. It was a perfect blend."

Hmmm, sounds like a musician right after a successful record has been cut.

But Brewer is right, of course. Things have to happen that way if you are to beat the best teams from all over the Southeastern United States. And things have to happen that way for a hit song.

The successful baseball orchestration began with the selection of the best players from five different high schools and two colleges. Sort of like an all-star band.

From Gainesville High came shortstop Scott Powers and outfielder Billy Wilson, a pair of prep All-Americans; pitcher David Coker, after a season at Georgia College; pitcher Gary House, outfielder Gene Edwards, second baseman Dwayne Wellborn and reserve catcher Bartley Wilson.

North Hall contributed centerfielder Mike Gailey, after a season at South Georgia College; infielder Ricky Satterfield; pitcher Tracy Bales and reserve Randy Glass.

From Johnson High came first baseman Jim Edwards and pitcher Todd Reed.

East Hall High sent catcher Kenny Anderson and little brother Doug Anderson.

And from Forsyth County High came a couple of cousins, pitcher Scott McWhorter and third baseman Jim McWhorter.

It's not easy forming a team of players who are accustomed to being rivals with each other. That's like hiring a tuba player from Germany and a violinist from Israel.

But Brewer made it work. If you don't believe it, ask teams from Carrollton, Covington and Savannah that fell to Gainesville in the state tournament. Then ask Orangeburg, S.C., Orlando, Fla., and Hamlet, N.C., all state champions, who were Post 7 victims in the Southeastern playoffs in Greer, S.C.

The national competition will be much tougher this week. But getting to the Legion World Series is a very big accomplishment.

It's like being asked to play "Wildwood Flower" with Flat and Scruggs at the Grand Ole Opry.

Luke Rushton, Young Harris inseparable

June 11, 1980

They laid Luke Rushton to rest last week at a hilltop cemetery overlooking the scenic area of the tiny mountain town of Young Harris, a place he dearly loved and never intended to leave. And now he never really will.

Little Young Harris Junior College could hardly be called an athletic factory. It's never been the type of place a man could earn a national coaching reputation for himself. But Luke Rushton did.

For 22 years Rushton coached basketball at Young Harris, and nobody, and I mean nobody, ever laughed at that dinky little gym or the teams that rose from there to state and national prominence.

Six times Rushton's teams won the state junior college championship. Twice they made it to the national playoffs. And each time they gave a good account of themselves.

Many players developed by Rushton went on to fine careers at larger schools and he himself had opportunities to move up in his profession. But I don't think Luke ever considered leaving Young Harris as a promotion. He was so attached and so much of a part of the place that they were almost one and the same. No, leaving Young Harris would have been a step down so far as Luke was concerned.

Even when the school could no longer afford to support a basketball program and the sport was dropped about a decade ago, Rushton remained right there.

Luke's accomplishments as a coach must be prefaced by the fact that his school never had much of a recruiting budget, and he pretty well had to take the so-called leftover players after the larger schools had already skimmed off the cream of the talent. And this was in the days when good basketball players were not as plentiful as they are now.

But he had a knack and a system for getting every ounce of ability and determination there was in a player, and sometimes even more.

To see and talk to Rushton for the first time, you would judge him to be almost anything but a successful coach. He was small, smiling and soft-spoken.

Plenty of old coaches down through the years have been described as "beloved." But if any of them ever truly were, it was Rushton. His former players swear by him as a person and a coach. A crowd of them were on hand for his funeral and some served as pallbearers.

But Luke had one characteristic that fits all coaches. He loved to beat the so-called "big" or "name" teams. When he did, he would smile, wink and usually remark: "Aw, we're just a bunch of ol' mountain boys who got lucky."

After Luke was no longer coaching basketball, his son Eddie grew up and became a fine player at Towns County High School. Luke always said he wanted to see Eddie play college basketball and get his college degree. In a kidding manner, Luke would say: "I want Eddie to play for a good coach. He can't play for the best coach, because I'm not coaching anymore."

Luke got his wish on all counts. Eddie went to North Georgia College and played well for Coach Bill Ensley. A week ago last Sunday night, Eddie graduated from NGC. The following Wednesday morning, while playing tennis with Eddie, Luke suddenly died on the court of a heart attack.

Putting grief aside, I have a feeling Luke wouldn't have wanted it any other way. He also loved tennis, and he taught hundreds to play the game.

Last week his former players carried him to his grave. That, too, was fitting. They'll tell you themselves, he certainly carried them lots of times in the past.

East Hall coach longtime winner

November 17, 1981

Being in the high school championship football playoffs might be new to East Hall, but Coach Jim Lofton is no stranger to winning.

Lofton, in his third season as Vikings' head coach, has had his share of glory in a 27-year career which started in 1954 at North Fulton in Atlanta and continued on to Dykes of Atlanta, Jefferson, Lee Academy in Auburn, Ala., and Springwood School in Lanette, Ala.

As a head football coach, Lofton has posted a record of 144 wins, 65 losses and six ties. He has won numerous championships, including an Alabama state title at Lee Academy in 1975.

Friday night Lofton takes his East Hall team to meet the always-strong Commerce Tigers for the Region 8-AA championship, the first football title game ever engaged in by an East Hall team in the 23-year history of the school.

Commerce is also no stranger to Lofton. During his 10-season tenure at Jefferson (1965–1974) Commerce was his biggest rival. Friday night will be the 11th time he has faced Commerce.

"We are in the midst of building a football program at East Hall," said Lofton, "while Commerce has had a successful program going for years. But we are happy for the opportunity to play them again. We feel we are a much better team now than when we lost to them earlier in the season. It's a challenge we welcome."

Lofton has steadily improved the program at East Hall. In his first season here in 1979, the team was 5-5. Last year the Vikings were 6-4 and missed out on the playoffs in the last game of the season. This year the Vikings are 8-3 and in the region championship game.

Jim Lofton is and always has been a positive person, and a desire to work in a positive atmosphere is what brought him back from Alabama to an area of Georgia he has always liked.

"I went from Jefferson to Alabama in the first place to get into school administration," Lofton recalls. "But in administration you have to deal with too many negative things. I found I still wanted to coach and still loved the positive aspects of athletics such as working with young people and watching their development."

"I looked over some coaching opportunities back here in Georgia and decided on the East Hall position because I like this area, and I like the Hall County school system's attitude toward sports."

An added athletic joy for Lofton is the fact that all five of his sons have played for him. Son Bobby, now a ninth grader at East Hall, starts in the defensive backfield on this year's team, and the youngest, John, is involved in eighth-grade football.

In fact, it's a family package deal. Lofton's wife, Ruby Jean, also teaches at East Hall.

Lofton, who has a masters degree in education from Emory University and graduated from Auburn where he attended on a football scholarship and played on the 1954 Gator Bowl team, sees good days ahead for East Hall football.

When asked about East Hall's reputation as a basketball school where so many good athletes play only basketball, Lofton said that situation is changing because young athletes now involved in the junior programs are playing more than one sport.

"At a school our size," Lofton said, "you have to have your good athletes participating in all the sports they can if your overall program is going to accomplish anything. We think such a situation is developing here."

Lofton's success at East Hall this season is rather amazing when you consider he has only 21 players on his varsity squad. "But they're 21 dedicated kids," Lofton quickly points out.

Cursed, jinxed and snake-bit
December 15, 1982

Call it what you will. Fate, voodoo or just plain bad luck, but something always went amiss each time Coach Bobby Gruhn of Gainesville High got near a state football championship.

One of the most successful coaches in Georgia high school history, Gruhn and his excellent teams were speared by destiny not once, not twice, not three times but on four appearances in state title games.

The latest disappointment came just one week ago when Gainesville lost the state championship game to Bainbridge, 7-6, in a wet, muddy quagmire on the floor of Gainesville's City Park Stadium.

Neither team could hold onto the wet ball. Fumbles were numerous on both sides, but Gainesville's miscues hurt the worst.

Bainbridge's only touchdown came after a fumble recovery at the Gainesville five. On what proved to be the winning extra point, the holder fumbled the snap but managed to get the ball on the tee just in time for the kick.

Gainesville's only score came in the fourth period when Olaffie Hester returned a punt 48 yards for a touchdown. But a fumbled snap prevented the extra point.

Both teams spent most of the game just trying to hold to the football.

It was just another frustrating loss for the Elephants in a state championship game.

Gruhn's first such near-miss came back in 1968, on another wet night at City Park, when St Pius of Atlanta took a 6-0 win.

However, this was a somewhat legitimate win for a St. Pius defense that did not allow Gainesville even a single first down.

The following season, Gainesville was right back in the state title game again, this time against North Springs.

In a thrilling offensive battle, the North Springs quarterback broke a 75-yard touchdown run with three minutes left to play for a 28-21 victory.

Then in 1972, against Southwest DeKalb, the Elephants appeared to score the winning touchdown on the runback of a pass interception, but a penalty nullified the play.

With time running out, Southwest DeKalb blocked a punt and threw a touchdown pass in the final seconds for a 16-12 win.

They say elephants never forget.

Elephants on those four teams will certainly never forget.

Such losses are just too easy to remember.

High school basketball overdone?

May 25, 1983

The recent resignation of Billy Ellis as head boys' basketball coach at Johnson High could serve to remind us that we might well be overdoing things a bit in our high school basketball programs.

After 15 years as a head coach, the last seven at Johnson, Ellis just plain got tired. He makes it clear he cherishes his close associations with the young athletes and he will miss that the most. But his personal schedule—just as with many other high school coaches—simply got too demanding.

Now, let me say Billy Ellis never mentioned he thought high school basketball is being over-emphasized. Basketball has taken up most of his 37 years and he loves the game.

However, I believe the game definitely is being over-emphasized on the high school level. It has become an almost year-around thing for both players and coaches. It is a keep-up-with-the-Jones deal. If a coach is to compete and keep his job, he must do the things the competition's doing.

This includes a long, long schedule—with a holiday tournament thrown in—spring practice; spring games and then—of all things—summer camp and summer games. This is the way the system works these days.

"I never intended to coach for life," Ellis said when he announced his resignation. "I've been thinking about giving it up for quite a while now. In basketball, you practice before the season, during the season and after the season. You practice over the Thanksgiving holidays; you practice and play over the Christmas holidays; there is spring practice and summer programs. I just got tired. I decided to do something that would be a bit more fair to me and my family."

Ellis will remain at Johnson as coordinator of the work-study program in the vocational department. There was a smile in his voice when he said, "At least now I might be able to get home before dark sometimes, and I might be able to enjoy some of the holidays."

You see, high school basketball teams hold game scrimmages against each other in these various camps. It's not unusual for two teams, from entirely separate sectors of the state, to meet each other in state tournament after having already battled a number of times during the summer.

Summer high school basketball has become a very big thing. Coaches feel if they don't take their teams to these camps, they fall far behind the opposition and won't be able to compete when tournament time rolls around.

I believe if you happen to have a good enough team and good athletes who maintain an average practice schedule, you will still win, summer camp or no summer camp. On the other hand, if you have a team that lacks talent, attending all the summer camps in the world is not going to "create" a championship team.

It seems unfair to the young people involved to take much of their holiday time and summer vacation time in an attempt to win more basketball games.

Life itself, after basketball is all over, will be tough enough for these kids without turning their games into full-time jobs while they're still in high school.

Cassell closes celebrated career

March 17, 1990

One of Georgia's legendary high school basketball coaches, Glenn Cassell, is retiring after 38 years and more than one thousand victories.

Cassell, for the past 13 years successful head coach of the East Hall Vikings' boys basketball team, leaves with some impressive numbers.

During his career his teams won more than 1,200 games against 502 losses.

He won five state championships while coaching at Vienna High School before coming to East Hall, and he is the only boys coach in Georgia ever to be named National High School Association Coach of the Year.

During his stint at East Hall, his teams won nine region titles and made three trips to the state Final Four.

One of Cassell's biggest local wins came in December of 1983 when his Vikings ended the 33-game winning streak of the arch-rival Gainesville High Red Elephants.

Gainesville was fresh off a perfect 30-0 season and a state championship when East Hall took the 70-67 win at the East Hall gym. East Hall's Stacy Thomas, bound for the University of Tennessee, led the big win along with Philip Cronic, Jeff Borders and Ricky Whelchel.

It was the only loss suffered by Gainesville that season as the Elephants went on to a second straight state championship.

Upon retirement, it was typical of Coach Cassell to downplay his many wins and championships when he said he "considers the associations formed with his players" as the most important achievement of his career.

A peerless performance

July 17, 1994

A career milestone has been reached by yet another outstanding Gainesville sports figure.

Don Brewer is observing his 20th consecutive season as head coach of the Gainesville Post 7 American Legion baseball team, and he has no peers so far as his coaching record is concerned.

Coaching in a town well known for a rich tradition of athletic success, Brewer adds his name to an impressive list of championship coaches.

Under Brewer, Gainesville Legion teams have literally dominated the Georgia competitive scene.

Brewer's teams have won more than 600 games, an average of more than 30 wins a season, while gathering seven state championships, 14 area championships, a Southeastern Regional championship and a trip to the American Legion World Series.

It was in 1979 that Brewer's team became the first Georgia team to ever reach the World Series and went on to attain a fourth place finish in that exclusive event.

But Legion baseball is not Brewer's only arena of success.

A native of North Carolina, Brewer is a graduate of East Carolina

University, and has a masters degree from North Georgia College in Dahlonega.

Brewer first arrived on the Gainesville scene as coach of the Gainesville High School basketball team.

In 1974, he took his GHS team all the way to a berth in the state tournament, the first such trip for a Gainesville basketball team in 14 years.

Brewer also coached the Gainesville High baseball team for six years, and in 1975 his Red Elephants posted a 24-8 record, won a North Georgia championship and advanced all the way to the state finals.

Brewer also took a short fling at college coaching when he was named head basketball coach at Gainesville Junior College.

Brewer left GJC to enter private business, but his love of coaching kept him attached to his American Legion baseball position.

In 1984, Brewer survived a serious health scare when he had to undergo surgery to correct nine heart blockages.

He battled back and made a rapid return to his coaching duties.

Well aware of his heart condition long before his surgery, Brewer for years was a dedicated runner, and experts say his physical condition probably saved his life.

Scores of athletes who played under Brewer went on to college careers and some of them advanced to the professional level.

Jody Davis, who played 10 years in the major leagues with the Chicago Cubs and Atlanta Braves, played Legion baseball under Brewer as did Cris Carpenter who also made it to the major leagues.

Brewer's many years of community service were recognized in 1988 when he was named recipient of the Gainesville Kiwanis Youth Service Award.

Brewer's record, hundreds of athletes and the fact that he is alive, all attest to his dedication.

Gruhn let others take credit

September 10, 1995

In the overly visible world of sports, the late Bobby Gruhn was a rarity. He was, to the end, a totally selfless man.

Despite some 40 years of success as a coach of athletic teams at Gainesville High School, ego was never a problem with the usually bashful Gruhn.

In fact, if Gruhn suffered from any personality flaw, it was a failure to believe that any accomplishment was due to any talent on his part. Oh, cerainly Gruhn was well aware that most of his teams were winners, and that a grinding work ethic led by him was the main reason.

But to Gruhn, hard work and dedication to the program at hand were simply a natural part of the job. He never saw himself as a driven taskmaster or setter of lofty goals.

He was a working high school coach who believed that both preparation and luck were equally important. And he never argued with the fact that one or the other was responsible for both wins and losses.

Gruhn, who just Sunday died of cancer at age 66, was somewhat of a legend among Georgia high school coaches.

He came to Gainesville High as an assistant coach in 1954, became head football coach in 1963 and held that position for 30 years.

Most coaches who become big winners are usually lured to other locations. But Gruhn spent his entire career at Gainesville High.

He had other offers. But he loved Gainesville. He would never have gotten comfortable anywhere else.

Before he was named head coach here, he personally didn't think he would get the job. When he got it, he didn't think he would be able to keep it.

But he weathered some early storms and became a winning fixture at the tradition-rich home of the Red Elephants.

He was best known as a football coach who, during one span starting in 1966, posted 23 consecutive winning seasons and numerous championships. But he also had success coaching basketball back in the 1950s and also directed a number of state champions in golf.

Along the way, he has been named Coach of the Year in Georgia, Man of the Year in Gainesville, served as president of the Georgia Athletic Coaches Association, coached a North Georgia All-Star team and coached the Georgia All-Stars to an upset win over the Florida All-Stars.

When seriously pressed on the subject of personal success, Gruhn always replied, "Heck, I've just been fortunate to coach in a town with a rich high school football tradition that usually produced dedicated young players. And I've always been lucky in having some very fine assistant coaches."

You can't go through public life without making some enemies. But Gruhn made very few, and even then he certainly didn't do it intentionally.

Through it all, Bobby Gruhn remained Bobby Gruhn. Something of a foot-shufflin' good ol' boy who, when praised, always seemed to be saying "Aw, shucks."

CHAPTER 7

BASKETBALL
PROVIDED FOR ALL

Basketball was the game of the masses because it included so many levels of competition for anyone interested in taking part.

The red shoes

March 5, 1959

High school basketball players never had it so good. With new gymnasiums going up all over the state, the prepsters of today usually perform in more spacious surroundings than ever before.

They shoot at nylon-cord baskets suspended from the most modern glass backboards. They're sure of true bounces while dribbling on gleaming floors that cost $20,000. Electric scoreboards and clocks inform them of the exact score and time left to play. Heating systems maintain the correct temperature.

While watching recent tournaments being played in a high-class atmosphere created by the above conveniences, we couldn't refrain from thinking back—not too many years ago—when things weren't so plush.

When teams gathered for a tournament in those days, many of them came from schools that had only farms for a playing area or no indoor court at all.

There was a formula for picking the top teams that usually worked. Spectators would watch for those players whose basketball shoes were covered with red clay.

The presence of the mud was a sure indication of three things: (1) the boys played and practiced on outdoor, dirt courts most of the time; (2) they probably were forced to shoot at homemade hoops without baskets, and; (3) they were accustomed to passing the ball most of the time because the dirt playing surface was too rough for much dribbling.

Teams came in from places such as Tate, Ball Ground, Jasper, Marble Hill and all points north.

They came with their homemade uniforms with numbers sewn on the jerseys by momma's hand.

They came with their dirt-stained basketball shoes tied together and hanging around their necks.

They came and they played hard for the honor of Canton, Ellijay and Braselton.

The dirt-court boys usually came up with the toughest teams to beat in tournament play. They were fast as lightning on a hardwood floor and their passing game was extremely accurate.

This is not meant to hail "the good old days" nor to knock today's performers. But the lads of a few years back certainly were forced to make more of a sacrifice for the right to participate in athletics.

It is hard to pick a tournament winner now because the days of the "red shoes" are gone forever.

The big swish

December 25, 1960

The evening of Thursday, Feb. 5, 1953, might well be remembered in state prep basketball circles as the night of the "big swish." For it was on this date that a slightly-built Hall Countian accomplished the phenomenal feat of scoring 88 points in a single game.

This wholesale basket-burning still stands as a Georgia high school record and probably will until someone invents a bombsight for basketball players.

It's only fitting that the man who set the record is still in the basketball business. He's Don Parks, the pleasant and quiet young coach at Lumpkin County High in Dahlonega.

Parks' torrid performance seemed to fit right in with a rather wild season that year. Local cage rivalries were hot and numerous disputes and official protests resulted. On the national scene, legendary Bevo Francis was shattering scoring records for little Rio Grande College.

Parks stuffed the scorebook with his 88 points while playing for old Sardis High against Gillsville at what is now the Gainesville junior high gymnasium.

Like most athletes, Parks vividly remembers his big night and the circumstances leading up to it.

"The whole thing came about as the result of sort of a duel between Medley Odell of Oakwood High and myself," Parks recalled recently.

"I had scored 53 points against Lula one night and people began to say I had set a record of some sort. Then Medley scored 55 points in one game and I wanted to beat it."

"That night against Gillsville, I set out to get a lot of points. It was the final game of the regular season and we won by something like 127-36. Not too many high school players had perfected the jump shot at that time, but Medley and I used it and I also had pretty good luck with a hook shot. It seemed like everything I threw up there that night went in."

Parks was not perfect. He missed one shot, a 10-foot attempt in the final quarter. He hit 35 out of 36 field goal attempts and 18 straight foul shots.

He remembered one incident with a chuckle. "Gillsville played a man-to-man defense and they put a different guard on me in the second half. We were coming down the floor and my guard said seriously, 'I wish you'd slow down.'"

As we said, it was a season for the unusual. One one occasion, Odell and his Oakwood mates defeated the University of Georgia freshman team. Sardis played Truett-McConnell Junior College on two occasions. One member of the

139

TMC team was Parks' brother, Bobby, who now coaches at White County High in Cleveland.

Class C Sardis played a schedule composed of Class C, B and A teams as well as TMC and Parks averaged 33.3 points per game for the season.

Don went on to play for Truett-McConnell and averaged 20 points per game for two years. He still holds the school's first and second individual game records with 45 and 39 points. After playing at Piedmont College, he returned to TMC as coach for two years, and one of his teams set the school win record.

Parks' appearance hasn't changed too much since he was a 5-10½, 149-pound senior at Sardis. Many of his ex-teammates and opponents are still performing in the amateur ranks, but Parks apparently feels he can't improve too much on past performances and prefers the coaching ranks.

Parks now has his Lumpkin County Indians rolling on a winning streak and is enjoying it, but it is not probable that anything in the field of basketball will ever overshadow the night of the big swish.

The quiet world of Jimmy Wood

February 22, 1967

Jimmy Wood of East Hall High School is an exceptional young man. He is an A-student, a basketball star and a popular guy with his classmates.

On the surface, you might say there is nothing unusual about this since many teenagers fall in the same category. But, you see, Jimmy Wood cannot hear.

He is a 17-year-old senior who attends a high school where everything is geared for students who must be in possession of all their senses if they are to keep up with today's fast-paced education and athletic programs. Despite his handicap, Jimmy has not only kept pace; he is far ahead of most.

You would never know Jimmy is under any type of handicap from watching him perform on a basketball court. He averages about 14 points per game and has been a starter for two seasons. A slender lad, he stands six feet and weighs about 165 pounds. He shoots well from outside, has smooth, deceptive moves and is an excellent feed passer.

Says East Hall Coach Dub Jones: "Considering Jimmy's grades, attitude, ability and desire, I would say he is one of the finest all-around athletes we have ever had at East Hall. I can certainly say I have enjoyed coaching him as much as anyone."

How does young Wood perform so well without hearing? First, he gets his instructions from Coach Jones through lip-reading. Pure instinct helps

m react to many situations on the court and watching the movements of the
her players tells him when the whistle has blown.

East Hall uses about five different offenses and defenses. Jimmy
emorizes the sequence of the systems and usually makes changes without
fficulty. However, if there is any deviation, teammate Melvin Garrison is
signated as the man to give Jimmy hand signals which denote a switch.

Had East Hall fielded a varsity baseball team last season, Jimmy would
ave been an outstanding player, according to Coach Jones. "Jimmy is a good
tter and can play any position. He did well in Little League."

The son of Mr. and Mrs. J. D. Wood of Cornelia Highway, Jimmy comes
y his athletic ability naturally. His father, who carried the nickname "Fuzzy"
his younger days, was a fine second baseman for New Holland in the old
eorgia-Carolina Industrial League.

Before Jimmy entered high school, it was suggested that he be sent to
special school for the hard-of-hearing. He would have none of that. He said
e wanted to give it a try at East Hall. He had the confidence that he could
ake it and he was right. Especially strong in English and history, Jimmy's
verage for four main subjects last year was 96, 90, 88 and 86.

He gets his class lectures through lip-reading and is a member of the
ey Club and Letterman's Club. Because of his hearing, Jimmy also has a
peech impediment, but this does not prevent him from taking an active part
classroom debates.

There was some opposition to the writing of this article. One skeptic
aid readers might think the story is intended to generate sympathy.

Nothing could be further from the truth. I have only admiration for
immy. I reserve my pity for those of us who have full use of our senses and
aculties and still do not accomplish as much as those of Jimmy Wood's breed.

Ageless Ben keeps hookin'
'em in

March 6, 1968

When you see him perform, it is immediately obvious that Ben Martin
s a basketball player from another era.

All around him, the young and sleek athletes soar high into the air and
aunch deadly jump shots from far outside.

Then there is Ben—spindly and high-hipped, dribbling around near the
asket, dodging and faking to find an opening through taller defenders. He
uddenly rolls away from the bucket and lets fly with an old-fashioned hook

141

shot that loops high over out-stretched arms and sighs through the netting with a gentle sound no louder than a pygmy blowgun.

Ben Martin's basket counts the same two points as the more modern and spectacular jumper. If seniority had anything to do with it, Martin's would count more because he is 43 years old and has been playing basketball for 3 years. Still taking part in recreation and amateur leagues here, Martin consistently scores above 30 points per game. He is an ageless marvel.

"I'll keep playing as long as I enjoy it and it doesn't bother me physically," says Martin who is transportation director for the Hall County school system when he's not firing that hooker on a basketball court some where.

Although he fooled around with some outdoor games as a kid, Martin really didn't play any serious basketball until he was 22 years old. He didn't finish high school until he had served with the U.S. Army in Germany in World War II. He was too old to be eligible in high school, and his real career started quite by accident while he was attending Young Harris College.

"I was just playing around with a group in the gym one day when the basketball coach saw me and asked me to come out for the team," recall Martin. "I did and played there for two years."

Martin averaged about 17 points per game in those days when team totals seldom reached 40 points. He went on to play at Presbyterian College and Erskine his junior and senior years.

When he finished college, he began playing with Chicopee in the old and very strong industrial league in 1950-51.

He competed in the annual textile tournament at Greenville, S.C. where some of the finest amateur basketball teams in the South once gathered. He was selected on the All-Southeastern team and newspapers there referred to him as "a former Erskine star." "That was funny to me," Ben laughs. "I didn't average playing but about five minutes a game at Erskine. certainly wasn't a star."

But Martin has been a star in these parts ever since. He has played with numerous amateur teams since that time. "I remember plenty of years when guys like me and Maxie Skinner (former Piedmont Little All-American would get up a team and just go hunt tournaments to play in," says Martin.

Ben says the most notable changes in the game since his college days are the accurate outside shooting and the size of the players. "We almost never used to shoot from outside," he says. "And when you had a player 6-4, he was considered a giant but few of them that size could move very well. Now fellows taller than that can run with a fast break."

Martin coached high school teams at Lyman Hall, South Hall and North Hall for 10 years. He considers Bud Lunsford, who played for him at Lyman

[all, as the best all-around player he ever coached. Lunsford now is on the
ame amateur team with his old coach. Martin says Gerald Cochran of North
[all is the best shooter he ever had.

Ben admits that he still plays old-fashioned basketball. He seldom
hoots from outside and the antique hook shot remains his best weapon. "It's
s good as an other shot if it goes in the basket," Martin smiles. The hooker
as gone off Ben's fingers and into the basket countless times down through
he years. He has scored as high as 47 points in a single game and no one in
hese parts has yet discovered an effective defense against it.

Years from now—when basketball players are even bigger, faster and
etter—Ben Martin will probably be right out there with them, twisting, turn-
ng, faking and jacking that ol' hooker up there.

Basketball, by George

December 14, 1971

George Sorrell is only 18 years old, has played in just 11 college basket-
all games and already is causing quite a stir in Georgia junior college
ompetitive circles.

Sorrell is Gainesville Junior Colleges' freshman forward who last sea-
on at this time was helping Berrien County High School of Nashville, Ga.,
oward a State Class AA championship. In his brief career with Coach Bubba
3all's GJC Lakers, he has already attracted more attention than the town
drunk at a church social.

An amiable, smiling youngster who never appears ruffled even under
ressure game conditions, Sorrell currently is the leading junior college scorer
n the state with an average of around 27 points per game and also ranks near
he top in rebounding and percentage shooting.

Endowed with great jumping ability, the 6-5, 190-pounder soars high to
laim rebounds and block shots. He has the body control to pin opposing layup
ttempts against the glass without committing a foul. In other words, while
perating inside where it is always crowded, Sorrell is quick, graceful and
smooth as black silk.

Sorrell is just one member of a deep and talented Laker team. Although
ne has been singled out game after game, his teammates are unselfish toward
him. Many times they may have a shot of their own, but will feed inside to
George for the higher percentage chance.

Young Sorrell is well aware of this. After being named most valuable
player in last weekend's Christmas Tournament, which the Lakers won at

143

their gym, George didn't hesitate to say that the other players were respons[
ble for his receiving the award.

Sorrell's demeanor on and off the court has gained him quick popularit[
A veteran official said of him: "I've made two bad calls against him and h[
didn't even complain about those. He just plays basketball."

With Sorrell doing his thing—combined with fine play by Lakers Bi[
McAlister, Sherman Cornelius, Chick Ludman, Alonzo Patterson, Leonar[
New, Pat Donohue, Dave Jackson and William Moore—GJC has a six-gam[
winning streak and an 8-3 record.

With a long season still ahead, no one can say just yet how well th[
Lakers will do so far as the overall junior college schedule is concerned. Bu[
the team is definitely proficient and entertaining.

The Lakers don't resume action until Jan. 3, but local fans should pla[
to avail themselves of the opportunity to observe this team and the abilities [
George (Silky) Sorrell.

Basketball gospel

May 19, 1974

High school basketball in these parts won't be quite the same anymore[
because colorful Ford Phillips of Dawson County High School is leaving th[
coaching ranks.

After 24 years of tutoring prep basketball teams, Coach Phillips off[
cially steps down today when a program honoring him is held at the hig[
school in Dawsonville at 3 p.m. Phillips will continue as athletic director an[
teacher at the school, but his small, feisty, bantam rooster form will no longe[
be seen on the sidelines.

For almost a quarter of a century, Phillips has led three useful lives a[
teacher, coach and Baptist minister. Whether he conducted a class, a game, [
funeral, a wedding or a church service, Rev. Phillips did them all with intens[
dedication to the cause at hand.

Now 61 years of age, Phillips says he will leave the coaching game t[
younger men. "I enjoyed coaching," he said on the phone Saturday. "I enjoye[
being with the children and trying to teach character along with winning. [
especially enjoyed seeing the youngsters happy, and winning made them
happy," he laughed.

Coach Phillips taught a lot of youngsters a lot of happy basketball
because his overall record shows that his Dawson County boys' teams won 74
per cent of their games and his girls' teams were winners 72 per cent of the time

He carried at least six teams into state tournament play. His good teams were known for their speed and outside shooting ability. Some of the finest long-range bombers in the area were taught by Coach Phillips. Among them were sharpshooters such as Gene Odom, Rodney Robinson, Woody Bowen, Bobby Storey, Don Waldrip, Ford's own son, Jimmy, and many, many others.

Coach Phillips looks back and rates the late D. B. Carroll as probably the finest girls' basketball coach he ever saw. Carroll had state championship teams at both Forsyth County and Jasper High. Phillips also praises the abilities of Maxie Skinner at Banks County, Harold Hammondtree of Forsyth County and Clarence Dennard who had some fine teams at old Chestatee High.

Coach Phillips also remembers some tough basketball encounters in boys' play with Red Hitchcock of Jackson County, Don Wade of South Hall and Dub Jones, formerly of East Hall.

"Basketball has changed a lot since I first started," said Phillips. "But I believe the biggest difference is that so many teams now play a slower, more controlled game designed to take short shots. We all used to play the run-and-shoot game with lots of outside shooting. I was fortunate to have a number of good shooters."

Phillips, who will stand and talk basketball with anyone for hours on end and never tire of it, was entertaining to watch during his games. He was a mobile coach, getting up and down on the sidelines, pointing, yelling instructions and getting totally involved in the contest. No man could look more pained when things went bad, or be happier when things were good. The play on the floor was always reflected in his expressive face.

Phillips began his career as a teacher in 1932 at Cross Roads Elementary School in Forsyth County. He was 18 years old at the time. Now, 42 years later, he continues on in the classroom and the pulpit. But he is leaving basketball.

Congratulations, Coach Phillips, on a fine career. All the outside shots taken in the future by Dawson County players will be in your honor.

Brotherly basketball

February 9, 1975

If someone remarks to North Hall basketball player Jody Davis that "big brother is watching," he can take it literally.

You see, Jody's big brother is Jerry Davis, the head basketball coach of the North Hall Trojans who carry a fine 16-6 record into the Region 8-AA West Tournament at the Gainesville High gym Monday.

Jerry, who played his prep basketball at old South Hall High, ha coached his younger brother through three seasons of varsity play, and ther have apparently been none of the problems that sometimes result from suc an arrangement.

At the beginning, Jerry was not too sure how things would work out. " knew I was going to have to be careful in certain situations. I didn't want t be too critical of Jody, because I think an older brother tends to lean more i that direction. But so far as I can tell, there have been no problems whatsoeve so far as the other players are concerned."

Coach Davis speaks of his players as a team when he says he is "please with their efforts" this season.

The word "team" has had to be the key to success for the Trojan because they are definitely smaller than the opposition and have a winnin record because they work well together, make a minimum of floor mistakes take high percentage shots and use their quickness to make steals and forc turnovers.

Jody Davis, a 6-3 senior, averages 17 points and 13 rebounds per game He is by far the biggest man on the team but works well with his smalle mates.

Tim Oliver and Greg Williams, who both stand 5-11, each average 1 points in scoring and both do a creditable job on the backboards considerin their height.

Two little men, Doug Satterfield and Mark Gailey, stand only 5-8, bu are quick as tiny pickpockets operating in a rush-hour crowd. Satterfield aver ages scoring 11 points a game and Gailey averages eight, mainly because he i prone not to shoot very much.

During the regular season, Williams stole the ball from the oppositio 47 times and Satterfield came up with 42 swipes. Reserves Doug Glenn an Gary Hatfield have come off the bench for good spot performances.

Jerry Davis is regarded as one of the best high school coaches in thes parts, and his team can be a threat in tournament play, especially when th Trojans go into their Arabian Nights act known as "Jody Davis and the Fou Thieves."

Remembering Dan Reeves

January 23, 1977

Sometimes it's rather strange how an event of the present can trigger memory of just a routine happening of years ago.

146

When it came to my attention that a fellow named Dan Reeves is being considered as the new head coach of the Atlanta Falcons, it suddenly came to me that I first heard of Dan Reeves when I was covering the State Class A high school basketball tournament in Macon back in March of 1961.

Oh, I certainly remember Reeves as a dependable and versatile running back for the Dallas Cowboys and before that as a quarterback of some note at the University of South Carolina.

Then, only yesterday when I heard Reeves is supposedly in Atlanta this weekend talking with Falcon owner Rankin Smith, did I recall my brush with Reeves some 16 years ago.

A number of our area prep basketball teams, including the Commerce Tigers, were in Macon for that state tournament. The Tigers, who were led by a quick little fellow named Billy Hendricks who now coaches the Commerce team, were to meet Americus in a first-round game.

Trying to get a little information on the Americus team, I talked to a fan who said: "The Reeves brothers are the boys to watch on our team. Bobby Reeves is the best, but his brother Dan just always seems to do a good job even though he doesn't look like he can. He's just a fine competitor."

That fan turned out to be so right. I think Bobby Reeves got about 19 points and Dan 17 as Americus quickly eliminated Commerce in the first round, 71-39. Americus went on to win the state championship that year and the Reeves brothers were the big reasons. In fact, the final victory was over Winder-Barrow, 52-47.

Dan Reeves was not widely recruited by the colleges, but at South Carolina he had a total offense figure of more than 3,000 yards. He didn't get drafted by the pros, but he signed on with the Cowboys as a free agent and was a valuable player on some of their fine teams.

It appears that throughout Reeves' career, he has been underrated, and all he has done is be a winner wherever he has played.

I don't know if he will get the Falcons' coaching post, but if he does, the selection will be criticized because everyone seems to think Atlanta needs a name, proven coach.

I recall Reeves in 1961 as a hustling, serious high school basketball player who had to work hard to get the job done. But he was always a big factor in the game.

During an interview when he first became a candidate for the Falcon post, Reeves quipped: "I was raised in Americus which is nine miles from Plains. I remember before the days of Jimmy Carter, Plains used to be nine miles from Americus."

Someone asked me how I can remember a minor event back in 1961. That ain't nothing. I recall the year before that when a pretty young gal named

147

Nan Jared was a cheerleader and fine basketball player for Gainesville Hig School. She is now Mrs. Jody Powell, wife of the press secretary for Presiden Jimmy Carter.

Julius jumps to the big time

March 9, 1979

It's a long leap from a backyard on Spring Street in Lula, Ga., to th polished hardwood of the NCAA basketball Mideast Regionals, but that' exactly the accomplishment of Julius Brown who made a memorable stop a East Hall High School here along the way.

Brown is now an outstanding member of the Middle Tennessee Stat University team which will compete in the Mideast Regionals of the nationa college basketball playoffs against Detroit University at Baton Rouge, La Sunday at 2 p.m.

The fact that Brown has made it to the big time is not really surprising despite some moments of indecision along the way. Ever since Julius' mothe Mrs. Julia Brown, provided that outdoor goal in Lula, basketball has been way of life for Julius.

Now comes reward time—the honor of performing in the center ring collegiate basketball. Brown is believed to be the only local high school prod uct ever to do so.

Brown's Middle Tennessee State team is somewhat of a surprise entr because it had to upset favored Austin Peay in the finals, 77-65, to win th Ohio Valley Conference championship and earn the trip to the NCAA playoff

At 6-4 and weighing 190, Brown starts at forward and averages 12. points per game. He leads the team in free throw shooting with an 86 per cen mark. He hits on 48 per cent of his field goal attempts which is excellen because he favors those long, ripping jumpers he used to pour through for th East Hall Vikings.

Middle Tennessee has a small, quick team with all five starters averag ing better than 12 points per game. It carries a 20-8 record into the regiona and Brown played in all 28 games.

Jim Freeman, the Middle Tennessee athletic publicity director, said b phone from Murphreesboro, Tenn., "Julius had just a fine year for us and wa a big factor in our success. His attitude is excellent and he is very popular wit his coaches and teammates. We're all happy he decided to come here."

Actually, Julius decided twice to go to Middle Tennessee. When he fin ished a fine three-year career at East Hall, he picked Middle Tennessee. The

he changed his mind and went to the University of Georgia where he turned
n some solid play as a freshman. But he changed his mind again, transferred
o Middle Tennessee, had to sit out one season and got back in action in 1976.
Certainly the NCAA berth makes him happy he made the move.

Brown first attracted basketball attention here when he played in the
Gainesville-Hall County Boys' Club junior leagues. He was as good as everyone expected at East Hall where he averaged over 20 points a game over four
seasons.

In his senior year as a Viking, he averaged 25 points a game, set two
school scoring records and led Coach Eddie Waldrep's team to a 27-2 record. In
he opening game of the 1973 State Class A tournament at Macon, Brown
destroyed a Jenkins County team when he bombed in 35 points, most of them
on that long, beautiful outside jumper of his.

But in the second game of the state tournament, a huge Monticello team
knocked the Vikings out. Brown got 18 points that night, but Monticello's size
was just too much. One of the reasons for the East Hall defeat was the
rebounding of a big kid named Ulysses Norris who distinguished himself as a
ight end on the University of Georgia's Southeastern Conference football
championship team last season.

Middle Tennessee's stay in the NCAA tournament might be brief
because that Mideast Regional bracket also contains nationally-ranked
Michigan and the University of Tennessee.

But brief stay or not, Julius Brown has made it, all the way from
playing those long hours in that backyard in Lula.

Demise of a hot-dog hoopster haven

December 2, 1979

When the old Candler gym burned down last week, a few generations of
basketball players had to feel a twinge of sadness.

The rustic structure, believed to be close to 50 years old, was probably
he site of more basketball games of all types than any similar facility in these
parts.

Built with WPA labor out of materials donated by farming citizens of the
Candler community, the building was characterized by inside support columns
which were simply pine logs with the bark stripped off by hand. The place was
a work of rural art, and in its early days was heated by two pot-bellied stoves
at each end of the court, with power provided by a sputtering Packard automobile engine.

149

Although I played in a number of get-up games there back in the 1940's, my most vivid memories of the place were provided by a so-called amateur tournament, the Candler Invitational, played there each March in the late 1950's and early 1960's.

The Candler Invitational was a montage of basketball talent. Teams which entered were a conglomeration of street players, high school kids, grizzled industrial league veterans and some college stars from schools such as Georgia, Tech, Oglethorpe, Furman, Clemson and all the area junior colleges.

The game they played was strictly a hot-dog affair. Run and gun, put it up from anywhere, score, score and score some more. It was a showcase for shooters, ballhandlers, dribblers and runners. You got the feeling if anybody played defense, it was a technical foul.

I remember the youngsters firing up those deadly jump shots, as opposed to some of the older players who preferred the hook and even two-hand, underhand set shots.

It was not unusual to see some teenager from East Hall High School going one-on-one against ageless Glenn Turk who could still muscle it up on the backboards at 42 years of age.

Team sponsors brought in ringers from everywhere. Godfrey's Service Station of Jefferson was usually the University of Georgia varsity. Stell Photo of Winder might be a collection of Clemson and Furman players. Nix Ford of Cleveland could be composed of a collection of junior college standouts. They came and played under team names such as Roper Hydraulic of Commerce, Gainesville Iron Works, Harris Lumber of Canton and many, many more.

There was the year Bud Lunsford, destined for car racing fame, led all scorers despite the presence of some big college names.

Some who went on to college coaching played there, including Bill Ensley of North Georgia, Roger Couch of Georgia State, Wayne Dobbs of Vanderbilt and Johnny Guthrie of Georgia.

I remember the night Maxie Skinner, who a few seasons before had made All-American at Piedmont College, scored 27 points in the first 12 minutes of a game. Everyone thought he would get 100. But although his shooting eye was still there, his playing shape left something to be desired and he tailed off to something like only 44 points.

There were the basketball families, such as the Odell brothers—Medley, Charlie, Tony and Stan—who played together.

There were showboats galore like veteran Bill McClure who could dribble blindfolded through traffic all night, and two of my favorite hot-dog names, Leon Luckey and Ludon Rockamore.

Ah, but an interesting era ended when the stuffy NCAA stepped in and

uled that active college players could no longer participate in such extra-
urricular activities. It seems the NCAA felt some of the collegians might be
etting paid for their services. I'm sure a bit of travel, meal and beer money
might have exchanged hands, but certainly nobody made any profit. It was all
or fun, and fun it was.

But when the college boys went, there went the thrill local fans got
when "one of their own" could outhorse a player who made the headlines.

How a simple fire ever brought down Candler gym I'll never know. I've
seen it withstand a lot hotter performances than that.

National title a dream, a reality

March 24, 1980

Back during the regular basketball season, the National Junior College
Athletic Association had the Truett-McConnell Danettes ranked as the number one women's basketball team in the nation.

Such a lofty rating for a team from a tiny Baptist college in the hills of
North Georgia brought some cynical smiles, and someone even remarked that
Coach Colby Tilley of Truett "must know someone with some pull at national
headquarters" in order to get the rating.

I remember asking Coach Tilley about that at the time. Colby, a low key,
soft-spoken, nice guy type, stated flatly, "I not only don't know anybody out
there, I don't even know what criteria they use for rating teams. I assume they
go by won-loss records. It's nice to be rated number one, but it really doesn't
mean very much because there'll be a national tournament. Some team will
win it and be the real number one. I just hope it's us."

Last Saturday night Colby's hopes came true. His Danettes became
number one in the nation the hard way, by beating the other best teams in the
nation.

The Danettes' march to the national title was no easy tip-toe through
the tulips. It was tough.

First, Truett had to dispose of the top teams right here in Georgia and
they did that, including a couple of key wins over a very good Gainesville
Junior College team.

Then they had to take on the best from the state of Florida and kept
moving by disposing of Miami-Dade South to reach the national playoffs in
Overland Park, Kan.

Just before departing for the national tournament, Coach Tilley vacated
his humble image long enough to say: "When we went to the national tourna-

151

ment two years ago and finished seventh, we were happy just to be going. But this year we are going with the intention of winning it all."

Then they proceeded to do just that.

The Danettes opened with an 83-61 win over Western Wyoming as Truett's Robin Hendrix, a tall young lady from Kokomo, Ind., with the eyes of a gypsy dancer, scored 43 points and took down 18 rebounds.

The next night, the victim was Henderson, Tex., 72-63, as Hendrix, destined to become the tournament's most valuable player, got 18 points and 21 rebounds. Martha Moss, a sweet-faced gal from Towns County High in Hiawassee, delivered 18 points. Back during the season, it was Moss, only a freshman, who stepped in to fill a void left when Robin Rainwater, a star most of the season, was lost for the year due to an injury.

In the Friday night semifinals, the Danettes had to face Northwest Mississippi which had a perfect record of 32-0, and the team that had taken over Truett's number-one ranking. Mississippi fell, 60-57. Moss struck for 19 points and Stacy Byrd, a Gwinnett Countian with a bright smile, scored 14. Hendrix had foul trouble and was held to just seven points, but she scored four of them in the last five seconds to pull the games out.

In Saturday night's national championship game. Truett won it all with a 63-61 thriller over Cloud County, Kan., a team taller than a row of healthy corn. Another freshman, Tina Ingle, an all-around athlete out of Gibsonville, N.C., hit the two biggest free throws of her life with just eight seconds left in the game to provide the winning points. Hendrix sealed her All-America credentials with 29 points.

Now it's over, and Truett has that national championship Coach Tilley said they were going out to Kansas to get.

It doesn't make any difference who knows who at national headquarters. The ratings are a thing of the past for this year.

The Truett-McConnell Danettes are the REAL number one.

Royal reign of the Lady Vikings

March 26, 1981

Nobody in the history of girls' basketball in these parts ever went on a four-season run like Coach Seth Vining and his East Hall Lady Vikings.

Today is "Seth Vining Day" as proclaimed by the Hall County Commission, and they're giving Seth one of those old-fashioned country covered dish suppers out at the school cafeteria.

This is all in recognition of what Seth and his East Hall girls have accomplished over the past few seasons, including back-to-back state championships.

Vining signed up to coach football and baseball at East Hall back in 1975, but some changes were made and he became the girls' basketball coach.

It must have been fate, or destiny, or something like that, because it wasn't long before good things happened.

In his third season, Vining coached his girls into the state tournament.

Then, wham! His girls, led by the play of talented young women such as Linda Earls, Sylvia Akers, Dinah Latty and Brenda Hill, posted records of 28-2 and 26-4 and won two straight state championships.

Although some of the top players from the state title teams graduated, the Lady Vikings racked up a 25-5 record and finished runner-up in state play the next season.

The hot run brought much recognition to Coach Vining.

He was named Coach of the Year by the Atlanta newspapers, twice named coach of the year by the Georgia Athletic Coaches Association and was selected to coach the North Georgia All-Star team which defeated the South team.

The covered dish supper will probably be regarded as the biggest honor because it's being given by the home folks.

Our kids earned all-star spots

July 28, 1981

Supposedly the best high school basketball players in the state will be showcased at the Omni in Atlanta tomorrow night and both games will have a definite local flavor.

The Georgia Athletic Coaches Association is presenting its annual prep extravaganzas and Gainesville, East Hall, Johnson and White County will be represented by some talented individuals.

In the boys' game, flashy Joe Mintz of the East Hall Vikings and big Danny Watkins of the Johnson Knights will be on the North squad.

The girls' game starts things off at 6:30 p.m. and playing for the North will be mobile Kitty Rucker of the Gainesville Lady Elephants and tough Jeanette Dorsey of the White County Lady Warriors.

You never know in all-star games just who will be playing how much because the coaches tend to go with those players who happened to look good in the too-brief practice sessions, but everybody usually gets in some playing time.

No matter how our kids do in the one-shot game, all of them have proven they deserve to be there.

Many East Hall followers believe Mintz is the best all-around player ever to attend the home of the Vikings which has turned out more than its share of fine players. Mintz, who can do it all on a basketball court, led Coach Glenn Cassell's Vikings to a perfect record through the past regular season.

Coach Billy Ellis of Johnson swears by Watkins, a 6-6 leaper who helped the Knights all the way to the state Class AAAA quarterfinals in 1980. Watkins can score as well as get on the boards.

In the girls' department, Gainesville's Kitty Rucker played four years of outstanding basketball and shattered almost every female record at the school. An excellent athlete, Rucker last season directed Coach Buddy Bowman's Lady Elephants to a sub-region championship, one of the few titles ever won by a GHS girls' team.

White County's Dorsey was the main reason the Lady Warriors won the state Class AA championship last season for Coach Wicky Loudermilk who finally won the "big one" after so many years of trying.

All-star games never prove very much, and I don't guess they're supposed to. They serve mainly as final recognition for a job well done by youngsters on the high school level.

Just tip it off and give it a go, kids. This is your last high school fling, and in high school, it's all supposed to be fun.

Big Red runs to perfection

March 13, 1983

It was a perfect ending to a perfect season for Gainesville High School's undefeated basketball team.

Winning their 30th consecutive game without a loss, Gainesville took the State Class AAA championship at Macon Coliseum Saturday night by holding on at the end for a 75-69 victory over Mays of Atlanta.

Gainesville, with its running attack working beautifully, dominated the game for the first three quarters and appeared on the way to an easy win.

But in the fourth period, Gainesville had some starters in foul trouble. Mays got incredibly hot shooting the basketball, and at one time pulled to within three points of the Elephants.

Gainesville, however, got consecutive layups out of Patrick Hamilton and Cris Carpenter and then Terence Bailey hit a short shot with just 45 seconds to play to put Gainesville up 72 to 67.

154

Bailey, a six-foot-three senior, then added two free throws with just 19 seconds left, practically locking up the game because Mays didn't have time to catch up.

Just after the opening tipoff, Carpenter stole the ball, dribbled the length of the court for a layup. The Red Elephants never trailed again.

Gainesville led 19-13 after the first quarter, 37-26 at the half and 58-43 going into the final quarter.

The Wolves began to cut into the lead early in the quarter and Gainesville was guilty of some sloppy play that helped Mays catch up. But the Elephants maintained their composure in a close game in the final minutes and then celebrated the first state basketball championship in the history of the school.

Hamilton, a 6-2 junior, repeatedly drove the baseline and hit outside jumpers to lead Gainesville scoring with 20 points. Slick-passing Carpenter and leaping Charles Earles had 14 points each for Gainesville.

Bailey, always quiet but always steady, had 12 points including the four big ones at near the end.

Big Dennis Williams did a job rebounding and on defense and put in six points for Gainesville. Sub Randall Harper added two points.

Leading the way for Mays was Paris Dennis with 17 points and James Wilkins, younger brother of the Atlanta Hawks' Dominique Wilkins, with 16 points.

Living with number one

March 12, 1984

When Coach Jerry Davis' Gainesville High Red Elephants won their second straight state Class AAA basketball championship last weekend, they beat the jinx of being favored.

The Elephants posted their 59th win in their last 60 games when they ran past the Fulton Redbirds of Atlanta in the state championship finals.

Gainesville was favored in the game. The Elephants were supposed to win because they were defending state champs with star players Patrick Hamilton, Charles Earls and Cris Carpenter back from last year's perfect season.

But the matter of the difficulty of "living with number one" came up prior to the championship game.

After Gainesville defeated a good Decatur team in the state quarter-finals, Coach Davis was standing outside his dressing room telling members of the press how proud he was of his team's effort in the victory.

But an Atlanta sportswriter, with a devilish grin, remarked, "Hey, but you're ranked number one. You're supposed to win. It's news only if you lose."

Such is the pressure of being favored.

However, it must be said that Coach Davis and his Red Elephants have gladly brought it all upon themselves by being ultra-successful over the past three seasons.

In 1982, the Elephants posted a 28-2 record and barely lost to Decatur by two points in the state championship game.

Last year Gainesville went undefeated with 30 consecutive wins and won the state championship.

Coach Davis apparently enjoyed being number one because even before this season started he said, "We could be state champions again. I don't know if we will be or not, but I certainly think we're good enough."

And they were.

Yep, nobody really wants to be favored, but everybody wants to be number one.

Some say Brenda was the best

October 2, 1994

They called her Brenda (Sugar) Hill simply because she was such a sweet basketball player.

Hill, who stood 6-1, is regarded by many observers as the best female basketball player ever to come out of these parts.

Hill, who got her start at East Hall High School playing on two state championship teams coached by Seth Vining, blossomed on the college level with outstanding play at two institutions.

Brenda first took her sugary game to Auburn where she was All-Southeastern Conference in both 1984 and 1985.

She left Auburn in her junior year and later played at North Georgia College in Dahlonega where she made NAIA All-America, NAIA National Player of the Year and led NGC to the national finals.

She set NAIA national scoring records with 42 points in a single game and 115 points during the national tournament.

In her farewell season at NGC, she averaged more than 29 points and 12 rebounds per game.

How sweet can you get?

156

Basketball backgrounds Braselton buy

March 30, 1989

When they announced the other day that the tiny town of Braselton had been sold to a movie star, my mind immediately shot back a quarter of a century.

No, I didn't mentally delve into the background of the Braselton family. Neither did I conjure up the childhood of Kim Basinger, the actress who bought the town.

My thoughts went back to an unforgettable high school basketball team that represented the Braselton-Hoschton area 25 years ago.

Yes sir, I remembered the Class C state champions of 1964, the old Jackson County Panthers.

No doubt, the Jackson County Panthers of that season still must rank as one of the best small school basketball teams ever assembled in Georgia.

That team, coached by a guy named Bob Cooper, captured the attention of the state by posting a 34-1 record on the way to the Georgia title.

Longtime residents of Braselton-Hoschton today can recite the Panthers' starting lineup of Victor Stewart, Ronnie Hill, Jerry Eidson, Jimmy Waters and Larry Beck who played together starting in their elementary school days.

It was a somewhat amazing team in that Eidson, at 6-foot-1, was the tallest player. It was a team that could shoot from inside or outside and had the overall speed to dazzle you with a fast break attack.

And quickness carried over to defense where the Panthers, like busy little pickpockets, specialized in the stolen ball and always favored the pass over the dribble.

When they won their 25th straight game of the season, they did so by defeating the Hart County Bulldogs, who were the defending state Class AA champions. In that game, as an example of the Panthers' balance, Eidson scored 17, Waters 14, Stewart 13, Beck 13 and Hill 12.

Jackson County's only loss that season came in the Region 8-C tournament at Buford when Coach Ford Phillips' Dawson County Tigers pulled off a big upset.

Fortunately for Jackson County, it was a double-elimination tournament and the Panthers came back to beat Dawson County in the region finals.

Jackson County advanced to the state Class C tournament in Columbus and went on to the state championship by beating West Haralson 54-47; Jones County 57-54 in overtime; Calhoun County 57-56 in the final seconds; and Adrian 66-62 in the finals.

157

Jackson County's state tournament games were broadcast over Gainesville radio station WGGA. But at night, the station couldn't be heard in Braselton and Hoschton. So, those fans who were not at the tournament drove their cars to Blackshear Place, near enough to pick up the station on their car radios, and parked in a group to listen.

However, the story goes that on the night of the state championship, no one was left in Braselton except one member of the Braselton family who stayed home to look after the town.

And when the Jackson County team started home after winning the state championship, they were met in Lawrenceville by a 123-car motorcade and escorted the rest of the way to Braselton-Hoschton.

So, now Braselton is owned by a movie star.

Hey, I can remember when Braselton, and the entire surrounding area, was owned by a high school basketball team.

Sally's world is wide

July 2, 1997

Right at this moment, there are no more worlds for Gainesville basketball official Sally Bell to conquer.

When the new women's professional basketball league, the WNBA, opened play recently, there was Bell right out there with the pros doing what she has done for 19 years, callin' 'em like she sees 'em.

Being selected as an official for the pro game means that Bell has run the gamut of basketball officialdom. She has now done it all on all levels.

She has officiated just about all over the world for kids, amateurs, collegians, Olympians and now the pros.

Anyone who has followed Sally's career should have known she would be right there when the pros opened up.

She got her start like most, calling recreation and junior high games.

She advanced to the high school level here in the Gainesville area, then rose to the NCAA level calling national tournament games.

She has officiated in world championship and Goodwill Games play and has toted her whistle from Taiwan, to Spain, to Russia to Malaysia while doing so. And in 1996 she made it to the Olympics in Atlanta.

She has been honored along the way such as in 1991 when she received the Naismith Award, the highest honor possible for an NCAA official or coach.

And now Sally is calling on the bright, new pro scene.

I guess when the first basketball game is played on Mars, Sally will get the call.

CHAPTER 8

CAR RACING
A WAY OF LIFE

Whether it was old-time bootleggers hauling whiskey in fast cars over mountain roads, or legitimate racing on rustic dirt tracks and superspeedways, there has always been a love affair with fast automobiles.

Proof from the past

June 1, 1958

A musty, bedraggled archeologist has stumbled down from the hills of North Georgia bearing relics proving that the word *Enoche* is an old Cherokee Indian word meaning "sports car race."

We realize there will be doubters, but Professor Gascan P. Pitstop, after months of digging through the ruins of a Cherokee sports arena, has unearthed ancient signs pointing to this fact.

The new discoveries have brought joy to the hearts of the Gainesville Jaycees who sponsor the Enoche Sports Car Races to be contested on the runways of the Gainesville Municipal Airport this week. The Jaycees have long claimed they knew what they were doing when they selected the name.

Professor Pitstop, who we must admit was rendered a bit addled by his ordeal, first came up with a fossil that plainly shows the imprint of racing tires.

In a highly-secret seminar here, the good professor displayed a carburetor fashioned from a tree stump, a gas line made from hollow vines, flint-tipped spark plugs, valves and pistons made of rock, and large peas baked to hardness for use as ball-bearings.

But Pitstop did not stop there. Painted on the walls of well-preserved wickiups, he discovered drawings, that when translated, proved to be advertising for the annual Cherokee Grand Prix.

Through even more intensive study, Pitstop managed to reconstruct the final race held by the Cherokees.

Racing was rapidly becoming the national sport, said Pitstop, but a band of Spanish stragglers, who had deserted one of DeSoto's expeditions introduced gambling to the natives.

When every driver attempted to throw a single race, Pitstop related, the sport died, along with the Spaniards, and was never revived.

Professor Pitstop was carried away from the seminar by white-coated attendants, but he made a remarkable contribution to the lore of the hills.

Still in use today is a phrase coined by Pitstop. It says, "Gentlemen start your Injuns!"

Benny the 'swoosh'

March 9, 1966

"It was all like a dream. We just couldn't believe the good luck we were having. Everything went right for us and I'll never forget how good it felt."

These are the words spoken rapidly and with feeling by a young Gainesvillian named Benny Hawkins as he described an amazing seven days of drag racing success at big meets in Florida.

Piloting his metallic-blue, supercharged roadster in NASCAR events at DeLand and then the Winter Nationals at Spruce Creek near Daytona, Benny and his pit crew of Buddy Ralston and Donald Cain won just about everything it was possible to win.

"We went down there just hoping we might win at least one in our class. We didn't even think about some of the other things that happened. We just didn't think it was possible."

With Hawkins at the wheel and Ralston and Cain working magic with the machine, they not only won in their class at the NASCAR run, they won in their class at the Winter Nationals, set seven NASCAR records, picked up $1.000 in prize money and capped it all off by taking the featured Super Eliminator runs at both sites.

All this did not occur at the expense of weak opposition. On hand were some of the top speed lads from across the country. They were there from California and Ohio, true hotbeds of hot rodding. When Benny won, he beat the best.

There was adversity, but it was overcome through know-how tempered with determination. While running at DeLand, Hawkins' car blew a clutch and suffered other mechanical injuries. Benny was about ready to tow the car back to Gainesville. But Ralston and Cain wouldn't let him. They went to a nearby junkyard, searched until they found enough usable spare parts and got the roadster running again. It continued to win.

Then at Spruce Creek, a head gasket blew. Again Benny was about to call it quits. But Cain, a driver himself, convinced him that he could run without water. Run without water he did, and continue to win he did.

Yes, there was some luck involved. "Racing on the beach meant there was a lot of moisture in the air," said Benny. "Some of the others there just couldn't adjust to the atmospheric conditions which were different from what they were accustomed to. One of things was that a set of spark plugs was just about shot after two runs. We were prepared for this and changed plugs every two races. Some of the others weren't, and you can't just walk in any place and buy plugs for supercharged engines."

Hawkins gives most of the credit for his success to Ralston and Cain. "No matter what came up, they were able to adjust and get the car ready to go. They really know what they are doing."

Associated with and financially aided by Speed Shop, Inc. here, Hawkins fired his vehicle down the quarter-mile drag strips no less than 20 times during the two meets.

Benny is especially pleased with his wins in the Super Eliminator run which pit class against class. In other words, his 1,480-pound roadster with a fiberglass body was matched against the "dragsters" which actually are merely frames pushed by the same type engine but weighing about 500 pounds less.

The best run of all came at Spruce Creek where Hawkins fired down the course at a speed of 160.93 miles per hour in an elapsed time of just 9.1 seconds.

A little fellow in his mid-twenties, Hawkins talks about five miles per hour faster than he drives. He loves what he is doing and, like most legitimate drag racers, he takes great pride in his accomplishments because he built that finely-tuned and delicate piece of machinery which rockets him down the race course.

There were plenty of witnesses to Hawkins' success. Some 6,000 spectators showed up each race day.

Benny will never forget his Florida trip. If his opposition remember him, they will probably recall only a blue blur from Gainesville, Ga., that just went "Swoooosh!"

A winner 400 times

July 2, 1967

In sports or any other field, there is nothing like winning. The biggest expert on winning in our neck of the woods, Bud Lunsford, will be honored at Anderson (S.C.) Speedway Monday night because he is living proof that nice guys can finish first.

Charlie Mize, Anderson Speedway promoter, has designated the 100-lap racing card Monday evening as "Bud Lunsford Night" in recognition of Lunsford's "outstanding sportsmanship and driving ability."

Just how successful has Lunsford been? In 12 years of piloting stock cars on Southeastern tracks, he has won more than 400 feature events and 37 of his victories have come at the Anderson track.

No one person could be more familiar with Lunsford's accomplishments than Mize who has served as either track director, starter or scorer at the tracks where Bud racked up most of his 400-plus racing victories. He won 19 events the first year the Anderson track opened in 1963.

During his racing career, Lunsford has pocketed some $100,000 in prize money. This is truly a fantastic figure when you consider the size of the purses at many of the stops on the area stock car circuit.

Lunsford, a 31-year-old Gainesvillian, is an excellent athlete outside his race car. He is an outstanding amateur basketball player and maintains a high bowling average.

A good example of his driving ability is the fact that out of the hundreds of races he has run, he has been involved in only one serious accident. That occurred a few weeks back at the Canton Speedway when his auto went over a retaining fence. He spent a short time in the hospital but went right back to racing as soon as he and his car were sufficiently repaired. The impact of the wreck cracked Lunsford's protective helmet which he has worn while winning more than 300 of his races.

Bud, who is married, has one daughter and operates his own speed shop in Gainesville, has not allowed success and recognition to bring about any change in him. He remains a rather quiet, clean-cut and unassuming fellow.

I have yet to hear a harsh word mentioned condemning Lunsford unless it came from fellows who spent a lot of time eating dust and whiffing exhaust fumes left by his number 49 racer.

The special night for Lunsford is a nice gesture by Mize. Maybe it will serve to launch Bud toward another 400 victories.

A vote for Road Atlanta

May 21, 1969

A group of Atlanta businessmen are seeking to locate a $1,000,000 sports car racing facility in the Chestnut Mountain area of Hall County, and we should welcome them just as we would any other desired industry.

Known as Road Atlanta Inc., the group already has the backing of the Chamber of Commerce and is a class operation which wants to construct a closed road racing track for the purpose of competition between expensive sports cars driven by internationally known drivers.

The final decision as to whether the track may locate here is up to Hall County's five-man commission which will hold a public hearing on the matter at South Hall High School Thursday at 8 p.m.

Opposition to the track is already building up. All sorts of arguments against it are being voiced. Some are reasonable, but most are exaggerated and the products of misinformation.

The truth is, the good points of such an attraction far outnumber the bad. Our county can hardly do anything but benefit from a facility which will draw thousands of spectators, participants, technicians, mechanics, officials and persons with financial interests here for five or six weekends per year.

The people deeply involved in sports car racing are not shysters or con men. They can't afford to be. So much money is involved in the sport that they are obligated to do everything in their power to make their product acceptable and prevent it from being a hindrance or troublesome to the people who support or endure it.

It appears that one of the major objections to the track is the fact that races will be held on Sunday. If the dissenters will excuse me, this is a rather bewildering argument. We don't close Lake Lanier on Sunday. We don't close our golf courses on Sunday. We don't close our parks on Sunday. We don't close our swimming pools on Sunday and we don't close our mountain trails on Sunday. These are all recreational facilities and so is a sports car racing track.

The people who come here for the events will purchase gasoline, food, many other types of merchandise and reside for a short time in our motels. If met with hospitality, they will carry the good name of our county back to their hometowns. We strive to picture our area as a tourist attraction and this would be an excellent opportunity to further this cause.

Bearing all this in mind, no one could be naive enough to think that Road Atlanta Inc. desires to come to Hall County merely for the betterment of our community. They are businessmen and sportsmen endeavoring to establish a profit-making venture. But at the same time, they are doing all they can not to cause any major disruptions.

The cars that would race here cost from $25,000 to $50,000 each. They would be driven by men such as Dan Gurney, Phil Hill and others of their breed who are dedicated to their craft and have proven themselves in similar competition all over the world.

Are we going to tell these people that there is no place for them in our county? I hope not.

P.L. of Westport

October 31, 1973

The voice on the telephone was that of an unidentified, but highly irate woman.

"Why didn't you tell us Paul Newman is driving at Road Atlanta?" she shrilled. "I just heard he had a wreck and wasn't hurt! Thank God! Do you know where he is staying? Why wasn't it advertised he was going to be here?"

Turning on the ol' cool and calm, I attempted to answer the questions as intelligently as I could: (1) I didn't know myself that actor Paul Newman was to be at Road Atlanta; (2) no, I don't know where he is staying; (3) I'm not in charge of advertising for Road Atlanta or the Sports Car Club of America.

164

The irate voice again: "Well, you're some kind of sports editor, not knowing when Paul Newman is in town." CLICK!!

Had I been able to reply to that last remark, I probably would have said that I have never quite placed sports writing in the category of keeping up with the whereabouts of movie stars.

Besides, I doubt if I would have made any big deal about it, even had I known. I've seen most all of Newman's movies and enjoyed most of them, but that's about as far as I go in the awe department.

However, since it turns out that Newman is one of the some 450 drivers here competing for national sports car racing championships, I began to search through a pile of pre-race publicity which has come to my desk over the past few weeks.

Sure enough, there it was, on the ninth page of the 12-page entry list. Listed under race 16 for B Sedan, the 21st name down to be driving car number 75, a Datsun S10, sponsored by the New York Metro Datsun Dealers, was one P.L. Newman of Westport, Conn. Why, I should have recognized him immediately.

P.L. Newman of Westport, Conn.? Being a fan of interesting names, that one would be culled out with the Joe Smith's, John Jones' and Phil Jackson's.

The list of drivers entered at Road Atlanta contains much more fascinating monikers such as Kendall L. Noah, who parked his ark on Lake Lanier; Dave Ammen, who hopes he gets through the race without losing an "m." Tom Pumpelly, who showed up just in time for halloween; Louis Lingo, who can communicate with anyone, or Sebastiano Barone, who certainly must be an international lover.

P.L. Newman of Westport, Conn.? That sounds like a used car salesman from Bogart.

I guess I'm just venting my disappointment. For the life of me, I can't understand how a guy named P.L. Newman could do such a good job as a pool shark in the movie "The Hustler." I've had great admiration for pool sharks ever since they made a habit of taking my lunch money every day in high school.

I hope they get your Datsun fixed in time for the race, P.L. It's nice to see you're learning a trade in case the movies are replaced by political scandals.

Okay, lady, call me again. I'm ready for ya.

Tom Friendly's mad dash

May 14, 1978

They're gonna run a car race called a Can-Am Sunday at a track known as Road Atlanta that is carved around the side of a rural hill in picturesque Chestnut Mountain. I don't know why they didn't name it Road Chestnut Mountain. Just a foul-up in geography, I guess.

I really don't even know what Can-Am stands for. But auto racing folks are rather strange anyway. They run races right through the streets of Monte Carlo and Long Beach, Calif. Try that in your '66 Chevy and you'll get arrested.

By now, you've probably figured out that I don't know very much, or care very much, about car racing. I never could bring myself to look on cars or horses as athletes. Of course, I don't know any horses who like sportswriters, either.

But I do want to make it clear that I was on hand at Road Atlanta for the very first race ever run there, and it was a Can-Am. It was back in September of 1970 and I thought it only fitting that I take in at least the inaugural event at the new facility.

Now, 1970 might not sound like too long ago. But at that time, Jimmy Carter was running for governor of Georgia, Kraft Music Hall and the Smothers Brothers were big items on TV, and Bob Didier was the catcher for the Atlanta Braves. The night before that first Can-Am, the Atlanta Falcons beat the Miami Dolphins in an exhibition game when Harmon Wages threw a touchdown pass to Paul Flatly. Oh, yes, two guys named Nixon and Agnew were going around making speeches about "radical liberals" and "destructive activists." Wages is now on television trying to keep his hair from breaking, and Nixon and Agnew have self-destructed.

Anyway, back to that first Can-Am. It was something. It was really something. As the kids under the grease rack at the nearest Exxon station might say: "Gawd, Marvin, you shoulda saw that race!"

You see, none of the favorites won that race. In fact, none of the favorites even finished. It was like a demolition derby on a roller coaster, and none of the fat cats survived.

The big deals in Can-Am racing at that time were the bright orange McLaren cars. In fact, McLaren cars had won 19 consecutive Can-Ams going into the Road Atlanta race.

Internationally-known drivers, who ran with the jet set and sipped champagne from gold loving cups, were on hand. There was Dennis Hulme, Peter Gethin and Peter Revson. There was even a good ol' boy in the field, Lee Roy Yarbrough of stock car fame.

166

Thirty-one cars dug off from the starting grid. I know, because I was peeking out a small window in the press trailer where they kept the free beer. Well, somebody had to guard the beer.

Bad things began to happen almost immediately to all the famous folks. Those $50,000 machines began to spin out on the turns. Gear boxes, gaskets and transmissions—or whatever happens to race cars—began to burst. Some cars, just banged into each other and got knocked all out of shape.

Through all that dust and debris came a beat-up, little old yellow Porsche driven by Tony Dean, a 37-year-old used car salesman from a small town in England. He was a "fun" driver. A guy with no financial backing, a car with an engine half the size of the others and a speed at least 10 miles per hour slower. Tony was just along for the ride because he liked to drive race cars.

Seven laps from the finish, Dean inherited the lead and sputtered home the winner. Only 11 of the 31 cars finished. Dean couldn't believe it. Neither could anyone else.

It was like Tom Friendly, of Friendly Ford in Decatur, driving a used Nova off his lot and running Mario Andretti and Gordon Johncock into the bricks at the Indianapolis 500.

I haven't been to a car race at Road Atlanta since.

I figured, what the heck. I've already seen the most rare thing in auto racing, a big upset.

I doubt that Tony Dean's feat will be repeated at Road Atlanta Sunday. The guy who wins will be one of the ones who is supposed to win.

I'll just savor my memory of the day Tom Friendly beat the world in a cream puff, one-owner Nova.

Moonshine led to NASCAR

June 15, 1997

Modern stock car racing, now under the auspices of NASCAR, got its start because of a bunch of illegal whiskey runners operating right here in the hills of North Georgia.

Now high-tech, big money and the most popular form of auto racing in the world, the sport started out more than 50 years ago when daring guys who used to deliver moonshine in fast cars got together for some racing competition between themselves.

They earned their reputations as great drivers by eluding pursuing law officers.

167

Most of the liquor runs were made out of the North Georgia hills, where the moonshine stills were located, to the big buyers in the Atlanta area.

When they weren't making runs delivering white lightning to Atlanta, the drivers would sit around and argue about who had the fastest car and who was the best driver.

They would make bets, find a pasture or deserted road somewhere and hold informal races.

Some of the better-known runners back in the 1940's were Lloyd Seay, Roy Hall and Legs Law. All eventually got into the racing business as well as the moonshine business.

Seay became one of the greatest of the early stock car drivers in the South, according to a book named *Mountain Spirits* written in 1974 by Joe Dabney, a former managing editor of the *Gainesville Times*.

In 1941, Seay got one of his many racing victories when he won the National Stock Car Championship at the dirt track Lakewood Speedway in Atlanta.

But on the following day, he was killed by a cousin during an argument over a load of sugar to be used in the manufacture of moonshine near Dawsonville.

Seay raced and ran liquor in a 1939 Ford, and there is a bas relief carving of that Ford, with a photo of Seay attached to the window of the car, on Seay's tombstone in the Dawsonville Cemetery.

Almost to a man, the early big names of stock car racing were big names in the moonshine running business.

Stock car racing booms bigger than ever these days, but the moonshine business has all but disappeared.

But in the 1940's, the daring young men in their souped-up machines hauled about 50,000 gallons of white lightning into Atlanta each week, according to Dabney's book.

Dawson driver a challenger

January 15, 1978

A Dawsonville driver who placed 35th in the NASCAR point standings in his rookie season, is looking forward to more competition on the big time stock car racing circuit in 1978.

Bill Elliott, who began his NASCAR career in 1976 at Rockingham, N.C., finished his first year with a standing in the point system and an 11th place finish at the American 500 in Rockingham last fall.

Elliott began racing, he said, because his father George Elliott of the Dahlonega Ford dealership had always had a race car "of some type." Elliott's first racing experience came on independent tracks in Class B in 1974. After winning ten races that year, he moved up to Class A racing on the independent tracks at the end of '74.

At the end of 1975, Elliott said, his father bought a car from NASCAR driver Richie Penze. His first NASCAR race in the car was at Atlanta, but Elliott failed to qualify. "It was my first race and hard to get used to the speed—still not used to it."

At present, Elliott drives a '76 Mercury bought from driver Bill Penske. With this car during the '76 NASCAR season, Elliott raced in ten races with his highest finish tenth at Darlington and Charlotte. He was also running with probable rookie of the year Ricky Rudd at Talladega when Elliott's engine went out. Rudd went on to finish ninth in the race.

For the upcoming NASCAR season, Elliott plans to have two cars: his present model and another to race on a shorter track. With two cars, said Elliott, he can enter more races. Elliott will also be bringing his year of experience to Daytona in February.

The most important thing about racing, Elliott said, is to "run as hard as you can and finish the race." Of fright, he said: "You are but you aren't. You're concentrating so much that you can't be frightened."

Elliott's pit crew, also of local makeup, will hopefully be improved next, he said.

Last year's crew included his two brothers, Dale and Ernie. Others were Steve Reagan, David Sosebee, Clinton Chumbly of Dawsonville, and Ricky Minter of Atlanta. Mike Turner of Dawsonville also worked some of the races with last year's crew. The importance of the crew to a race is great, Elliott said. Ace crews, like those of drivers Petty and Yarborough, can change tires and fill the gas tank in a few seconds. Elliott said his crew was trying to get their pit time down to 19–20 seconds.

Tires are a huge expense, said Elliott. With tires costing $100, Elliott said he couldn't afford to change so often. Free tires are given away to top finishers and famous drivers. Elliott said that he had received free tires three or four times his first years. For those needing tires, one route is to buy used ones from drivers getting free ones: "They (drivers receiving tires) just keeping getting richer and you must keep spending."

Expense is the greatest handicap to Elliott, he said. His aim this year is "try to win enough money to keep racing the next one." As to whether he'll make racing his profession, Elliott will only shake his head and answer "wait and see."

Click-click, twin luck, that quick

November 21, 1983

If you were fast enough with your television dial last evening, you got to see two pieces of good fortune back-to-back with Dawsonville race driver Bill Elliott and the Atlanta Falcons as the beneficiaries.

As I clicked back and forth between the Western 500 NASCAR race on the Superstation and the Falcons-49ers games on Channel 5, I had no indication of what was to come.

In the auto race, it was getting near the end with Tim Richmond and Darrell Waltrip battling for the lead, Benny Parsons next and the epitome of gold ol' boys, Elliott, running fourth.

Hmmmm, I thought, *another fine race Bill, but it looks like no big cigar again*. Rain was falling and it appeared the race might be cut a bit short.

Flicking back to the Falcons, I saw Joe Montana in the final minutes driving the 49ers toward a winning touchdown that would edge out the snakebit Falcons once again.

Back to the car race. What's this? Richmond and Waltrip get side by side. There is a bump. Both cars get sideways on the wet track. Like two ice skaters arm-in-arm, they slide gracefully right off the track and into the wet grass and mud. Scratch the leaders with just four laps to go.

I don't know much about auto racing, but I knew enough to realize Elliott was in a close second place to Parsons and Bill suddenly had his biggest chance to win a major race.

Like an infield fan atop a van waving a beer can, I found myself yelling, "Now, Bill! Now!"

And now it was as Elliott gunned his Thunderbird, shot past Parsons and streaked out to a solid lead. As if on order, the rains came down hard again, the field was put under caution and Elliott gleefully drove leisurely home to the win behind the pace car.

My mind conjured up a picture of stock car fans all over North Georgia dancing, shaking their beers and spraying each other in joy.

Back to the Falcons. Montana was doing something Steve Bartkowski can't do. He was scrambling into the end zone from 11 yards out to score what would be the winning touchdown.

Back to the race. Elliott, in that delightful drawl of his, was talking from his car and saying how he couldn't believe he had won his first big one.

Back to the Falcons. Last play of the game. Atlanta trailing 24–21. Now Bartkowski was doing something he can do, throwing the football nine miles into a crowd and hoping for heavenly help. The ball caroms off a crowd. Billy (White Shoes) Johnson, who had slipped down, gets up, catches the deflected ball and fights his way into the end zone. Falcons pull a miracle and win.

However, the official closest to the play is standing with his foot planted inches short of the goal. He has made no signal. He looks over his shoulder and sees another official running up with his hands raised indicating a touchdown. The first guy is off the hook and backs out of whatever call he might have made.

Bill Elliott won his event through the pure circumstances of what auto racing is all about.

The Falcons won their game through pure luck.

They'll both take 'em.

Time and tears right for Doc
April 10, 1986

Gainesville race driver Doc Bundy lived his dream at Chestnut Mountain's Road Atlanta track the other day.

Bundy and driving partner Sarel Van der Merwe won the prestigious Camel GT event over the second place team of John Paul, Jr. and Whitney Ganz.

After years of disappointments and coming close, Bundy had tears in his eyes when he steered the winning silver Corvette into the winner's circle.

"I cried all that last lap," said Bundy, a former Road Atlanta driving school instructor who has been trying and trying for a home course victory.

Bundy received the cheers of the crowd and was voted the Driver's Cup Award by the news media.

The winning Corvette started on the pole as it has before, but had failed to finish either of the two races it started previously this year.

The car is basically a research and development vehicle for Chevrolet which is trying to find a car capable of competing on the IMSA circuit against the Porsches and Jaguars.

Van der Merwe drove the first hour of the race and then Bundy took over. Van der Merwe then came back and was scheduled to finish the race. But with less than 40 laps remaining, he radioed in that his shoulder was hurting and he would need Bundy to relieve him.

Van der Merwe did not admit it, but Bundy and the crew believe he did that to give Bundy the chance to win the race in front of his home fans.

Bundy won one other race in 1980 during the Sports Car Club of America runoffs, and since that time he has come close, but accidents and other problems robbed him of winning chances.

Bundy's tears of joy were proof of his happiest day of racing.

Elliott well deserves a book

July 30, 1988

There is a book out about Bill Elliott, the pride of Dawson County and the modern ace of the stock car racing world.

Entitled *Bill Elliott: Fastest Man Alive*, the book is an entertaining and detailed biography about Elliott's sparkling career, his North Georgia rural background and his company's evolution into a high-tech corporate operation.

Admittedly, the book market these days is flooded with glowing reports on various athletic and entertainment figures.

However, most of these books are obvious attempts to take advantage of the ever-growing trend toward instant hero and celebrity worship.

It has become a literary fad to cash in on the high visibility of public figures in this country.

An athlete can have one good season, or simply be a member of a Super Bowl or World Series team, and someone is going to hustle out with a book on his life.

But most such books are usually not worth the buying price, and the athletes themselves are not worth a book.

Such is not the case with the Elliott book. Bill's record-setting and winning accomplishments on the race track are well worth a book, as is the story of how he became a legitimately admired racing and folk hero.

This is because Elliott is definitely not a one-shot, flash-in-the-pan accomplisher. He first arrived on the big-time racing scene back in 1976 and has steadily, if not doggedly, risen to the status he now holds.

And the book is not about Bill alone. It is an Elliott family story because the close-knit family aspect truly is the meat of the story.

Also, the book touches on the many "just plain hometown folks" who maintain a close connection with the Elliott racing operation.

No doubt, all highly successful athletes attract what are known as "hangers-on" fans who adopt heroes and thrive on the "bask-in-someone-else's glory" syndrome.

But this is not the case with most of Elliott's hometown followers. They are relatives and old friends of the family who were there offering encouragement and moral support long before Elliott became known as "Awesome Bill from Dawsonville" and "Million Dollar Bill."

And the book does not dwell only on the bright side of Elliott's career. The low spots and the recoveries are also well documented.

It is all there, starting with a young Bill who used to tinker with car engines all the way to the adult Bill who has won more than $7 million in the risky world of making a race car go fast and stay together at the same time.

The mere fact that Elliott has repeatedly been voted racing's most popular driver by nationwide fans is close enough to make his career and life worth a book.

Even the book's author and publishing company contribute to the home state image.

It is written by Al Thomy, a longtime Atlanta sportswriter, and is published by Atlanta-based Peachtree Publishers, Ltd.

Yes sir, the Bill Elliott story is well worth a book.

CHAPTER 9

LAKE LANIER BROUGHT MORE THAN WATER

With Lake Lanier came competitive sports such as water skiing, bass tournaments and international Olympic boat racing.

Skiing farmer

July 5, 1960

An ill wind blew good-sized whitecaps into Gainesville Marina's beach cove Sunday afternoon, and water skiers found themselves tossed around like ping-pong balls in a washing machine as they competed in the third annual Lake Lanier Championships.

But the unfavorable conditions failed to prevent a diminutive Jackson Countian from claiming four of the 16 trophies presented, including the big one for overall champion.

Tanned Gus Johnson, a 22-year-old farmer who raises beef cattle and once played end for the Jefferson High Dragons, bobbed across the churning green water to win first places in the slalom, jumping and trick divisions. It took no close point-figuring for him to win the overall award.

Johnson, who stands 5-8 and weighs 145 pounds (he says he usually loses around 10 pounds each summer from skiing and farm work), has an athlete's build and an interesting skiing background.

"I've been skiing about nine years," he says. "I first started on a 15-acre lake on our farm. At that time I skied behind a small boat with a 25-horse motor. It was really different when I got behind more powerful boats."

Johnson is at his best in the graceful slalom event. His first competitive outing was in 1958 when he won the Lanier title. In '59, a broken ski rope and a cut foot were two factors which helped to prevent a repeat. But just a few months later, he copped first place in the State Jaycee tournament at Savannah.

Johnson must be classified as a "natural" water skier. He took up jumping only two weeks ago in order to prepare for this year's Lanier competition. With a chuckle, Gus relates: "I went over that ramp eight times in order to prepare for this year's Lanier competition. I fell just about every way imaginable."

But the amazing thing is, after staying up that first time, Johnson was almost perfect in 14 of his next 16 practice attempts.

Gus is an advocate of the single-handle rope while touring the difficult slalom course. When the one-ski fad first became popular, most skiers believed the double-handle rope was best. But time has proven them wrong. Says Johnson: "You watch the big-time skiers. They all use the single-handle because you can control your 'slack' much better. You get much more reach while turing a buoy. The double-handle is probably more fun for pleasure skiing, but the single-handle does the job much better in competition."

Johnson, who will be representing Lanier in the State Tournament at Augusta this year, still considers himself "strictly an amateur," but he is a terrific competitor and we wish him the best of luck and smooth sailing in his future endeavors.

A bass is not a fiddle

April 13, 1962

Fishing has never ranked high as a spectator sport, but I was enticed into the role of an observer during a short excursion onto Lake Lanier yesterday afternoon.

The whole thing started when Ed Little and Byron Mitchell—two Gainesville sportsmen who either know a lot about fishing or are very accomplished liars—figured a non-fisherman like myself would do well to accompany them and learn at least a little something about this popular pastime.

I told them I didn't know a goldfish from a whale and would be of very little use on an angling adventure. But they hurt my professional pride by accusing me of being a prejudiced sportswriter. I agreed to go.

My ignorance displayed itself before we had cleared Gainesville Marina cove. As our small craft bounced along, Mitchell asked Little if he had plenty of Lucky Strikes. Wanting to make myself useful, I immediately offered Mitchell a cigarette. This brought sneers. It seems a Lucky Strike, to a fisherman, is a plug rather than a smoke.

However, we soon arrived at a spot where Mitchell guaranteed there would be bass. (This is a fish, not a musical term.) I immediately learned that fishermen are notorious for uttering untruths to each other. I had heard Mitchell tell of this "favorite spot" to others, but the place we stopped was nowhere near the directions he had given.

As we dropped anchor, which consisted of a heavy rope wrapped around two large rocks, I sat shivering in the wind as my companions opened up what appeared to be two large lunch boxes. Inside, they resembled a kit carried by a novelty salesman. Staring up were weird science-fiction animals of all colors and protruding hooks. I was informed these were lures and plugs especially designed to attract fish. Why a fish would try to eat those things, I'll never know.

With a motion akin to that of a baseball pitcher, Mitchell and Little began flinging their lines out into the water. It wasn't long before Little stated: "There he is." I looked around to see who was coming. I saw Little tugging with a bent rod. "Okay, net man." Little said. It was here I learned that the middle man in the boat always serves as net man. Now I always thought a net man was one who played up close in a tennis match or was a goalie on a hockey team.

Then it dawned on me that Little meant for me to pick up a butterfly net in the bottom of the boat and nab the fish on the end of his bent rod. Amazingly enough, I accomplished the feat. The bass weighed something less than two pounds but Little seemed proud of making the first catch. "Sure is little," Mitchell snarled.

Taking a close look at the fish, I decided the devices used to catch them looked more appetizing. Before too long, 10 bass had been caught but three of them were thrown back. Although a number of different plugs and lures were tried, all the catches except one were made on that red and yellow thing called Lucky Strike. The other was hooked on a bright collection of material Mitchell referred to as a Turkish Nightmare. (This is not the true name but the lure resembles a Persian dancer with a ruby in her navel.)

A raw, windswept drizzle—enough to drive any sane person indoors—began to fall. But the fishermen went about their patient casting as if it were a lazy summer day. In this respect, fishermen are like golfers. The elements may keep you away from work, but never from pursuing your hobby.

Soon, the fish decided to ignore us and my hosts reluctantly decided to head in.

After truthfully telling Little and Mitchell how much I enjoyed the afternoon, I thought back over the trip and decided that I had experienced a better day than either of them. Although they ended up with nine fine bass, they had hooked a few more then allowed them to escape. But with the net, I had performed flawlessly.

The fishin' fireman

April 19, 1968

Joe Guyton started out fishing for exercise and is now recognized as one of the most successful anglers on Lake Lanier.

The veteran Gainesville fireman, who keeps hauling in lunker bass year after year, seldom misses making a good catch and yet he cared nothing about the sport when he started out 15 years ago.

"I had gained a lot of weight, up to 206 pounds," recalls Joe. "It got so every time we had a fire it would wear me out fighting it because I wasn't in shape. I really didn't care anything about fishing. I took it up for exercise and it worked. I lost down to 175 pounds."

How can you get exercise fishing? There is plenty of activity involved the way Guyton does it because he seldom uses a boat. He fishes from land and moves around a lot. Walking the shoreline and climbing up and down banks keeps him trim.

Joe cares plenty about fishing now and has the record to prove it. The biggest bass he has caught in Lake Lanier weighed more than 11 pounds, and he has brought in uncountable nine and 10 pounders plus numerous extremely

178

fine strings. Ask anyone who knows about fishing on Lanier and they will tell you Joe is among the very best.

"I really don't believe there is much skill involved in catching fish," says Joe. "The skill is knowing where they are and using the right equipment."

Guyton says this time of year, when the fish are spawning, almost everybody catches fish with little effort. But like all good fishermen, Joe can make fine catches even when fishing is rated "poor."

Guyton is pretty much a "loner" when it comes to fishing. He mostly fishes by himself and is reluctant to reveal his favorite angling spots.

"I remember I had some good places a few years ago and told a couple of my friends about them," he says. "They spread the word and pretty soon those good places were fished dry. And don't let anyone tell you this can't happen. It certainly can, so I don't tell too much about my good spots now."

Joe believes that most amateur fishermen make two or three basic mistakes. "Most of them use sinkers that are too heavy and floats that are too big," he says. "They make a few casts with equipment like that and scare the fish away."

Guyton prefers a small float and uses split shot as a sinker.

A laughing, pleasant fellow who enjoys a good joke about as much as he does fishing, Guyton says many fishermen also waste too much time at spots where there are no fish.

"All the time you hear about people who say they went out and fished a place for a long time without getting a bump," he says. "It doesn't take long to tell whether there are any fish around. You can tell after a few casts. If I don't have some luck early, I hunt another place and keep moving until I find them."

At 48 years old, Guyton has been with the Gainesville Fire Department for 20 years, and there is even more fishing in his future when he retires five years from now.

He says he plans to buy a camper and tour the famous fishing spots across the nation. "I'm going to see some of this country and stop off at famous fishing spots I've read about like Alaska and Wyoming," Joe says with firmness.

A part-time sign painter who also does some landscape pictures for relaxation, Guyton says if his pension money isn't enough for the trip, he will pick up sign painting jobs across the country to help finance his dream trip.

Joe is very definite about his retirement. He says he won't hang around a single minute past time for him to hang up his helmet.

"When my day comes, if there is not a new fireman here to ride the tailgate of that fire truck, it will leave here empty because I'll be gone," Joe smiles.

One thing is sure. The day that tailgate is empty, the fish across America had better find a hiding place because Joe Guyton will be after them.

The pros are here

March 23, 1972

Those strangers you've seen lurking about the fringes of Lake Lanier recently are bass fishermen. No, they're not ordinary, weekend line-snappers. They're professionals who fish for sport and money, but not necessarily always in that order.

They're easily recognizable. Most of them wear windbreakers covered in colorful patches somewhat like a stock car with STP and Autolite decals. They are here because of the $55,000 Lake Lanier bass tournament later this month and have spent the past few weeks "scouting" the lake for spots where bass are most likely to hang out.

If you've seen them pass in a car, most likely trailing behind was a unique craft known as a super bass boat; an expensive, fast, flashy water skimmer equipped almost with everything from sonar to nuclear-powered fish detectors.

The pros come from all across the nation, and many of them regularly follow a fishing tournament tour similar to that of professional golf. They study and experiment with the most modern techniques of purist fishing. No trolling or live bait for them. They go about it the hard way and even arm themselves with topographic maps so they can determine the lay of the land under the waters they fish.

They didn't travel all the way here simply to meet the "challenge" of fishing Lanier. The local tournament is billed as the "world's richest bass fishing tournament" and that $55,000 purse is the main attraction.

The fellow who hauls in the most poundage over the three days of the tournament collects a neat $10,000 dollars. Even a seventh place finish pays $1,400 and the entry fee is just $150. The event's single biggest catch pays $2,000 and someone will pick up $1,000 for the largest bass each day.

There will be the usual crop of "amateurs" in the field, but as in golf, the pros are the odds-on favorites.

I'm not a fisherman, but I started to enter anyway because I'm naturally greedy. However, the rules are very strict and everybody got mad when they looked in my tackle box and saw those old crank telephones and dynamite.

Gary and the Islands

May 22, 1972

Gary Player, the dapper, polite and strong little golfer from South Africa, visited the construction site of the Lake Lanier Islands golf course here yesterday and used terms such as "fantastic" and "beautiful" to describe the layout which is scheduled to open this September.

At present, the course is in its rough stages. Grass has just been planted and the fairways and greens are bare dirt. But the outline is there, running right around the shoreline of Lake Lanier. Just how competitive the course will be remains to be seen, but certainly there is no more scenic setting for a golf layout anywhere in the world.

"This is such a beautiful setting," said Player as he walked the holes and hit test shots off the now muddy tees. Dressed in golfing shirt and trousers of beige, with rubber boots instead of spiked shoes, Player trudged from hole to hole accompanied by a small entourage which included Art Davis and Ron Kirby. They make up the firm of Davis, Kirby and Player, Inc., which designed the $1-million course which officially will be 6,900 yards in length, but is capable of considerable adjustment with all holes having at least three tee sites and many of them four.

The lake itself, with constant boating traffic, is visible at almost all times from the rolling terrain of the course which Islands' officials hope will soon be the site of at lest one major professional tournament.

Player, one of the greatest golfers of all time and one of only four men who have ever won the British Open, U.S. Open, Masters and PGA tournament in their careers, was especially impressed with the 15th hole which will be the showcase of the championship course.

The 15th is a par three of 180 yards. The tee sits right on the shoreline of the lake, and the tee shot is all carry across a cove to a peninsula green. "Just look at that," said Player as he stood on the tee and pointed across the water. "Just imagine when there is white sand in the traps, the grass is green and you have those sailboats in the background. There will be no other golfing sight just like it in all the world." He then promptly struck a five-iron shot to the middle of the green.

Following Player's tour of the course, there was a press conference inside a tent near the Islands headquarters building. Once there, Player told an attending group: "You have a facility here to be proud of. It will be a place to get away from it all. I hate golf courses in cities with autos buzzing all around. This place is going to be fantastic. It will be a balanced course, one to challenge the top golfer, the lady golfer and the hacker. It will be flexible and the scenery is unmatchable."

181

Speaking with that very pleasing British accent of his, Player said seri ously: "My, all those golf holes around the water are absolutely magnificent."

The maintenance of the course will be in the hands of superintendent Allen Baston who for seven years looked after the Augusta National, scene of the famed Masters Tournament which is just as famous for the condition of its course as it is for the prestige of its event.

I must agree with Gary Player. His being a pro and I a hacker, we have different outlooks on the playing of the game. But the Lanier Islands course is going to be so beautiful, I will enjoy shooting 95 just as much as Gary Player will his sub-par rounds.

Ugly golf can be pretty

May 24, 1974

When your golf game is going bad, hardly anything can ease that pain of ineptness. But a group of duffers found the remedy this past week. We played the scenic new course at Lake Lanier Islands.

Bad shots normally are followed by a thrown club, a few blue words and a scowl. But when the surroundings are so beautiful, your concentration strays from your bad swing and the undesirable result.

Such is the case with the par 72, 6,119-yard Islands course which is destined to be one of the most picturesque, natural golf layouts there is anywhere.

Our golfing safari started out at the American Legion marina where eight of us boarded the houseboat of real estate magnate John Robinson. The diverse gathering made us ready for almost any emergency. There was super salesman Stan Davidson, Jim (Mr. Clean) Henson, attorneys Joe Sartain and Jack Carey, insurance claims manager Elmer Lyons, insurance adjuster Guy Gaither and a sportswriter whose golf game is so suspect, that he was along merely to ensure against a beer surplus.

The leisurely trip down the lake to the Islands complex, in perfect weather, was a relaxed study of unforgettable scenery which those of us who live near the lake tend to take for granted.

When we arrived at the Islands course, we split up into two foursomes and teed off in a blaze of hooks, slices, shanks and white golf balls splashing into the green waters of Lanier.

We hit some of the most impure golf shots ever struck by man or beast. Ben Hogan would have paled at the sight and fainted on the spot. But, as said, the beauty of the course was the main topic of conversation.

182

Even the side bets became incidental. The course is new and there is
ome final trimming to be done. But it has an abundance of grass, the greens
ould hardly be better, and as you walk the fairways that run along the lake
hore, you can't keep your eyes off the shimmering expanse of water, dotted by
white sails.

The course rolls over hills on every hole and is characterized by the
umber of times you must shoot across water. There is really no long carry
ver water anywhere, but the mere presence of the aqua has a psychological
ffect on weekend golfers.

The par threes are all rather short but extremely interesting. Playing
rom the white tees, the course is not overly long. But it is designed so that
when it is stretched back to the blue tees, it can become a championship test.

Two of the most interesting holes are the par three 15th and the par
our 18th. At 15, the tee shot is about 160 yards and all carry over a watery
ove to a peninsula green which appears to sit serenely and alone in the midst
f the lake.

Number 18 is a horseshoe dogleg left which requires a tee shot over a
ove and a second shot over another cove to still another peninsula green. The
ourse has rather tight driving areas and sand traps placed to gather in almost
ny errant shot.

Anytime I fail to break 100 and still enjoy playing, there has to be an
dded attraction. The natural surroundings provided that.

When the golf was over, we returned to the houseboat where another
nsurance man, former Gainesville High football coach Clayton Deavers, had
rrived, and was playing the role of chef and whipping up a salad to go with
n evening meal of steaks to be charcoaled on the front deck grill.

No such trip is ever perfect. The boat's generator went out, and we made
he two-hour trip back without lights in pitch darkness. But Robinson
managed to make it on dead-reckoning after we told him that if anything
appened, only the captain would go down with his ship. The trip wasn't as
ramatic as Humphrey Bogart towing the African Queen through leach-
nfested waters, but it did have its doubtful moments.

However, setting nautical difficulties aside, if you like pretty golf, even
when your game is ugly, try the Lanier Islands course. The view is beautiful
ven when your ball is slowly sinking out of sight.

The great Olympic coincidence

March 7, 1994

Back in 1990, when Atlanta was awarded the 1996 Olympics, there was a mad rush across North Georgia to climb aboard the venue bandwagon.

Gainesville and all other communities even marginally in the vicinity of Atlanta clamored for any tiny piece of the Olympic pie.

Community leaders in Gainesville formed all sorts of groups to explore all sorts of opportunities.

People in the news business in these parts started seeking out anyone who might have an Olympic connection in their background.

Reporters were out after that ever-desirable "local angle" for possible future stories.

An individual who emerged in Gainesville was a quiet, aging gentleman named Bill Fields who possessed a prized accomplishment. He was a former Olympic gold medal winner.

Fields had won his gold medal as a member of the winning U.S. Naval Academy rowing crew in the 1952 Olympic Games in Helsinki, Finland.

Because the sport of rowing was rather foreign to folks in these parts Fields' emergence as a past Olympic hero did not attract a great deal of attention.

However, the news folks did file his name away for future reference.

Actually, Fields was not at all surprised that his rather obscure sport was hardly recognized in these parts.

There was very little publicity given to the winning of his gold medal even back in 1952.

It was certainly a very big deal in international rowing circles, but there were no ticker-tape parades for those who pulled oars to power long, skinny boats.

But in the world of rowing, that Naval Academy team is still regarded as one of the greatest ever.

It won 29 consecutive races in collegiate competition, and then won 14 straight Olympic events to take home the gold medal.

At the time Fields' identity as an Olympic athlete was first revealed locally, there was no talk of a rowing event here.

When there was finally some discussion about possible water events on Lake Lanier, it was revealed that rowing was to take place in Rockdale County where a lake was yet to be built. It was then that real pressure was applied to have some events on Lake Lanier.

Then, in December of 1993, it was announced that there would be Olympic competition on the waters of Lanier, and one of those events would be rowing, Bill Fields' sport.

184

However, there was some sadness involved in the happy announcement because Fields was not around to enjoy it. He had died some months before Lake Lanier was chosen.

By chance, the specific site for the events was within viewing distance of the Fields' home located in the Clarks Bridge Road area.

It's truly amazing how much bigger the sport of rowing has become in these parts since the "great Olympic coincidence."

CHAPTER 10

FAMILY, FRIENDS, ACQUAINTANCES AND HOLIDAYS

There was a time in the newspaper business when it was considered unjournalistic to write in the first person about family and friends, or to get too soppy about holidays. But most writers soon found that such use was often the best way to spin a tale.

Francis and the fifties

January 11, 1974

Francis Tarkenton's appearance as quarterback of the Minnesota Vikings in Sunday's Super Bowl is proof of the argument he has been putting up in his own defense for years.

Tarkenton spent most of his 13-year pro career with the Vikings, then an expansion team, and the New York Giants, a rather mediocre team. He was rapped as never being a big winner despite his outstanding individual statistics.

Now he is with Minnesota again and the Vikings are a solid team. Tarkenton himself says that the quarterback of a pro team is really not that important as an individual. Even a great quarterback can't win with a weak team. But wed him with talent, and a Super Bowl berth results.

A perfect example of this took place in 1955 when Francis (nobody called him Fran until he went north to the pros) was the quarterback at Athens High School.

Tarkenton was a junior quarterback behind a big, quick line and his backfield mates were super prep stars George Guisler, Billy Slaughter and Bobby Towns. The Trojans roared to the state championship, thrashing Valdosta in the finals.

During that regular season, Gainesville High and Athens played their traditional rivalry game at Sanford Stadium. It was no contest. Although the Red Elephants had a fine team led by quarterback Tommy Paris, the Trojans blistered the Elephants, 51-0, in one of the worst defeats ever suffered by a GHS football team.

Then came 1956, the year Don Larsen pitched the only perfect game in World Series history as the Yankees beat the Dodgers.

The Gainesville and Athens varsity teams met again, this time at City Park here, and Tarkenton was still the Athens quarterback. Ah, but there was a difference. All the horses who had played with Francis the previous season had graduated.

Tarkenton was brilliant in defeat. Gainesville had essentially the same team back and won by a 28-7 count as Paris, A. D. Watson, Theron (T-Model) Brown, Jack Bell and Richard Shaw battered the Trojans.

Tarkenton, Paris and Bell were to go on and play together on some fine University of Georgia teams.

So, you see, Tarkenton has always been a winner when given the proper tools to work with. Francis is a slippery, crafty little operator. But put him on a football field with no help, and he is like a master pickpocket with no fingers.

Having known and watched Tarkenton perform well in all sports since he was just a youngster in Athens, I would like to see him get a Super Bowl championship. But I'm afraid the Miami Dolphins will have a lot to say about that, because their tool kit might be even better equipped overall than Tarkenton's.

However, I can't see Francis lapsing into conservatism, as so many Super Bowl teams are prone to do. That just isn't his style as he has always been a flashy performer.

They busted Mr. Bill

July 20, 1975

There is a current controversy concerning the pros and cons of legalized gambling on sporting events.

I'm not going to go into all the arguments for or against such a project, because I have observed down through the years that people are going to gamble on most everything from pitching pennies to playing the stock market, legal or illegal.

Personally, I wouldn't risk a cent on the outcome of a ball game. I've seen so many sporting events that I'm convinced there is no way to know how any of them are going to come out, unless there is a fix on.

I do know that sports gamblers often have a very sentimental attachment to their pastime. They don't like to be criticized for taking part; they rationalize in agony when they lose and gleefully gloat when they win.

Most sports betting is sophisticated and impersonal these days. Gamblers use telephones and code numbers to bet with bookies they never see and subscribe to "tip sheets" through the mail to supposedly enhance their chances of winning.

There was a time in the past when bookies and their clients enjoyed an almost warm relationship.

Years ago, when the late Lee Crowe operated a pool hall down on Main Street, betting on baseball games was the big thing. Almost one entire wall of the poolroom was covered with a long blackboard which carried inning-by-inning scores of all the major league and Southern Association games. The information came in on a ticker tape machine.

One of the favorite bookies of the day was a quiet, kindly old gentleman referred to only as "Mr. Bill."

Mr. Bill kept tabs on bets placed with him by laboriously writing them down on a restaurant order pad with a stubby pencil. He went about his profession unobtrusively. He did not solicit business. It came to him. In a way, he was very pious about his job. He would not accept bets from anyone who was under age. He would also refuse bets from people he thought could not afford to gamble, especially if they already owed him money.

I can still see guys huddled around that tape machine and looking seriously at the results being chalked in on the blackboard. They would check the pitchers for upcoming games, mumble among themselves, make their decisions nod at each other and say: "Let's go find Mr. Bill." They never had to look far.

They would then go into quiet conference with Mr. Bill. They would tell him how they wanted to go and for how much, and Mr. Bill would listen, writing and nodding at the same time, until all bets were listed. The group would then break up; Mr. Bill would smile and wish them all good luck, and then stand and wait for more clients.

I never heard a harsh word uttered about Mr. Bill. Even the chronic losers liked him. He was good at consoling losers with soft words of sympathy such as: "Oh, that's too bad. You're just having some tough luck. You'll probably win next time."

Next time. That's a magic phrase to gamblers. There is always a next time.

Then it happened. One day some policemen came in with a warrant and took Mr. Bill away. The gamblers went into shock. They cursed everyone from the police, to the Mayor to J. Edgar Hoover. Why weren't the cops out catching murderers and thieves, they wondered aloud. It was a shame and disgrace

It turned out that the wife of one of the heavy losers got tired of her husband dropping his pay before he ever got home with it, so she blew the whistle on Mr. Bill.

The panic was only temporary, because Mr. Bill simply paid off a small gambling fine and soon was back in business. Of course, he had to lay low for awhile until things cooled off, and during that short period those gamblers were like the alcoholics going through the DT's. They were lost without their bookie.

I believe there is a bit of an urge to gamble in all of us. This was never more evident to me than the day they busted Mr. Bill.

Rocket fame or touchdown?

December 2, 1975

I saw the story right there in the newspaper today. It said that my old boyhood buddy, Bobby Bush, is now a renowned space figure.

The story said:

"A former Gainesville man, Robert A Bush, has been awarded an exceptional service medal by NASA, the National Aeronautics and Space Administration.

"A graduate of Georgia Tech and Gainesville High School, Bush was awarded the medal for his 'superior management of numerous disciplines and elements of the space shuttle program team.'"

"Bush has held key roles in the space agency for several years. He was in charge of the testing and flight certification of rocket boosters used in America's Apollo program which landed the first men on the moon.

"Bush is currently space shuttle project resident manager at the NASA national space technology laboratories, where engines of the new space rocket are being tested.'"

Ah, yes. Big time stuff for my old friend.

We were neighbors and pals for years on East Washington Street in Gainesville during the 1940's. We played football and baseball in streets and vacant lots. We delivered newspapers on bicycles.

The only time I saw Bobby show any interest in space in those days was when he ordered a telescope through an ad in the back of a comic book.

But it had nothing to do with the stars. Bush's house was located right across the street from the Brenau College campus. The telescope was strictly for girl-watching.

We went on to Gainesville High School together and Bush labored for long seasons as a reserve end on the football team. He didn't get into many games and was knocked around by the first stringers in practice. But he was a dogged, if untalented, competitor.

In the final game of the regular season in 1947, Bush had his closest brush with football glory.

Gainesville's Red Elephants, a great team that season, were beating the dickens out of the rival Athens Trojans on Thanksgiving afternoon at the University of Georgia's Sanford Stadium.

A senior ending a mediocre career, Bush got into the game in the final minutes.

Gainesville was threatening to score once again and tried a pass play.

Bush got clear in the end zone and a sure touchdown pass was spiraling into his eager and waiting hands.

Suddenly, out of nowhere, flashed the form of halfback Jack Roberts, Gainesville's great star. Roberts snared the ball for just another of his many touchdowns.

Bush was demolished by the incident after the game.

"It was coming right into my hands," he moaned. "I couldn't have missed it! My only touchdown ever! What was Roberts even doing in the game? What rotten luck!"

Now that Bobby is a famous space figure, a question crosses my mind.

On that Thanksgiving afternoon, in Sanford Stadium, with that touchdown pass floating towards him, what if a voice had suddenly said to Bush "You can catch this touchdown pass and enjoy momentary glory, or you can not catch it and go on to become a famous rocket scientist. What is your choice?"

Heck, I don't even have to ask Bobby about this.

Without hesitation, he would have taken the touchdown.

Jingle bowls

December 24, 1978

'Twas the week before bowl time and all across the nation, coaches were pondering their game situation.

Films were being studied with minute care, in hope some key flaws might be found there.

The players were all primed to a sharp degree, as they entertained visions of a holiday spree.

And Pepper with his Jackets eyed Perdue, wondering about the ankle of Eddie Lee Who.

When out in the Fiesta they raised such a clatter, as Arkansas and UCLA were to settle a matter.

I knew the promoters of each football event, would be counting the fans and each red cent.

Away to the bookie I flew like a flash, all too anxious to plunk down my cash.

The gambler was smiling past his gold toothpick; I knew in a moment it couldn't be St. Nick.

More rapid than eagles his handicaps he spoke, all the while glancing at my meager poke.

Now Orange! Now Cotton! Now Sugar and Rose! Bet it on anybody, Right on the nose!

Mortgage your house and bankers do call! Put it down boys, and I'll cover it all!

As loose money before the wild hurricane fly, I backed my favorite teams to the sky.

Then in case I hadn't been too wise, I looked at the bowls through the coaches' eyes.

I thought of Clemson and their fine quarterback, so betting on Woody Hayes I just couldn't hack.

I was awed by the desire of Dooley's men, but I wasn't so sure Stanford wouldn't win.

Then there was the magic of Notre Dame, while Houston's so fast it's a flamin' shame.

Penn State's defense can give you cramps, but Bear's boys are thinking national champs.

Southern Cal's Charley White has disco moves, but Michigan can punish like reindeer hooves.

Beware of Oklahoma's Billy Sims, he melts through your secondary like M&M's.

As over my wagers I began to sweat, I wondered if my bookie was still around yet.

But I heard him snicker as he snuck out of sight, "happy Christmas to all, I hope you bet right!"

Cabbages and things

November 1, 1979

The fact that Gainesville High plays Elbert County in a championship football game here Friday night brings back a memory of more colorful days when a lot of interesting characters lurked around the fringes of sports in these parts.

Back in the late 1940's, there was quite a bit of money bet on the outcome of high school football games. This is not true anymore, despite what you might hear from some people involved in law enforcement.

There was one guy in those days, we'll call him Robby, who would bet on anything that moved or stood still. Robby was a big, blustery guy who talked endlessly, had a big heart, worked for the state highway department, dabbled in politics all the time and could be deeply religious when it served his purposes.

Now deceased, Robby ran the gamut of lifestyles. He was a gambler, politician, trader in many merchandises and even once bought himself a big tent and hit the road as an evangelist.

Before we get back to his football connection, there is one story about Robby that must be told. During a gubernatorial election in the 1950's, Robby

193

worked on one of those highway department roadside weighing crews and wa. known as a fellow who could stir up some votes.

An aide to one of the candidates went to Robby and told him he woul be named to a supervisory position in the highway department if he would suc cessfully campaign for the candidate. Robby jumped in with both feet. H totally dedicated himself, plastered his car with posters and beat the bushe slapping backs and shaking hands for hours each day.

In the end, Robby's candidate won and took office.

Bobby wasted no time. He marched into the governor's office an demanded his big job. "Why, sir," asked the new governor, "What makes yo think you are qualified to hold such a position?" Robby turned red and boomed "Bless God, governor, I'm just as qualified now as I was the day you promise me the job!"

However, Robby didn't get the post and was frustrated about politic from that day on.

Now, back to football. One year Gainesville was playing Elberton in Elberton in a big game. On the afternoon before the contest, Robby entered pool hall in Elberton and made it known he would bet $300 on Gainesville One quiet little farmer in overalls replied that he'd like to bet, but that he ha no cash money.

"Well, just what do you have, sir?" asked Robby.

The farmer beckoned for Robby to follow him outside where he pointed to a pickup truck loaded with cabbages. He indicated he would put up the whole works against Robby's $300.

Robby circled the truck, checking it out and kicking the tires. He fondled some of the cabbages to check them for firmness, and announced the bet was on.

In a tough, close game that night, Gainesville pulled out a 12-7 win. Robby got someone to drive the pickup truck and cabbages back to Gainesville and sold both vehicle and load at a profit.

Someone asked Robby if he didn't feel a bit guilty about taking the farmer's livelihood. "Bless God," said Robby, "I prayed a lot about it and finally decided the Lord was using me to teach the good man a lesson."

There are few characters like Robby around anymore. They might have been unsavory to some people, but they certainly made things interesting.

My favorite athlete is 84

March 2, 1980

My favorite athlete will be 84 years old Sunday, And yes, he is a spry and active athlete.

He's my father, Lucius C. (Jack) Jackson Sr., a wiry, laughing little man of many friends and a familiar figure on the first tee at Chattahoochee Golf Club here.

Not only does he play golf about three times a week, and he plays well, he also works as the resident manager of a local apartment complex. In fact, work and play and duty and love all describe my father's active and interesting life.

Among my earliest memories as a child in the 1930's in the small town of Washington, Ga., was watching my dad play baseball, and he could run, hit and throw with the best.

Prior to my birth, he played what started out just as "town ball" between places such as Washington, Tignall, Warrenton and others, but it became known as the Million Dollar League. Money finally ruined it, as it usually does all so-called amateur sports.

Competition got so hot, a lot of cotton money was wagered heavily and "ringers" or "outside pros," were brought in to bolster the teams. When the players were no longer familiar to the townspeople, the league died.

My father was, and is to this day, a lover of most sports. Golf is his favorite and he was a scratch player in his younger days.

An auto mechanic much of his life, he even once raced cars when they wouldn't go much faster than 20 miles per hour.

He was a member of the Washington Volunteer Fire Department. I remember how exciting it was when he was awakened in the middle of the night and had to hurry out, break the glass pane out of the box on the front door of the firehouse to reach the key to open the door and ride off in that old red truck. Usually, it was to extinguish a blaze in the sawdust pile at the local lumber mill.

As a teenager here during World War II, I remember my father as chief of the Civil Defense Fire Department and how he so seriously would leap behind the wheel of that ancient American-LaFrance during air raid drills.

Among the fond memories for my two brothers and me were the many hours we all spent pitching baseballs back and forth in the yard, on the sidewalk or in the street with Dad.

There are many memories. Toddling along after him to the golf course...trips to old Ponce de Leon Park in Atlanta to see the Crackers

195

play... listening to baseball and football on the radio... sitting on his shoulders to watch circus parades... and even walking with him on bird hunts.

In the 1950's I even had the pleasure of playing on a civic club softball team with him. Nearing 60 years of age, his legs were not so quick, but he could still lash out those line drives at the plate.

Even today, he spins some of the greatest yarns about the old times in baseball and trips by wagon to games.

Among dad's playing companions was Tom Nash, a great football player at Georgia and still a member of the Green Bay Packers' all-time squad.

One of Dad's closest friends was the late Secretary of State Ben Fortson who was quite a boxer before an accident confined him to a wheelchair for life.

My father has helped to build two golf courses, one is now the Washington Country Club and the other is our own beautiful Chattahoochee Golf Club.

When Chattahoochee was only bulldozer tracks through the woods, my father was an unpaid worker helping it along. He was not the only one to contribute his time and sweat to have a course here, but he was among the most eager.

He was later to become course superintendent. A man with very little formal education because he had to become a farm worker at an early age, I remember him pouring over all the literature he could get his hands on to learn about golf course maintenance. And this was at an age when study and research did not come easy.

After we moved to Gainesville in 1939 and I was still not in my teens, I remember we visited back in Washington and we went to the golf course. A leading citizen of that town walked up on the first tee, spotted my father, stuck out his hand and said: "Why, there's Lucius Jackson! The man who could always do everything just a little better than anybody else!"

Most members of my generation like to knock the modern trend toward permissiveness where young people are concerned. They like to talk about how their fathers kept them in line with fierce physical punishment from belts, razor strops and the like.

However, in my personal case, I can remember only once in my entire young life that my father punished me physically, and I had it coming. I remember afterwards flopping down on my bed and crying. Then, someone was next to me, hugging me and also crying. It was my father. It had truly hurt him worse than it had hurt me.

To his granddaughters he is seldom known as grandfather, granddaddy or papa. They usually call him "Jack," and the name is spoken with love and respect.

The tales of the things my father has done and said in his long life could go on and on.

But I'd like to say he is not only my favorite athlete of all time, he is also the best man I have ever known.

Happy birthday, Dad.

Christmas list

December 23, 1980

Dear Santa,

My Christmas list for this year would be very difficult for even you to fill. Most of the things on it are from the distant past.

I realize some of these things might seem a bit silly for a grown man to request, but at one time or another, I owned them all. But, like the years, they just slipped away.

You don't really have to make an attempt to deliver them. It's enough for me just to get to write them down again.

So, here goes.

A Marty Marion shortstop glove and a Trapper first baseman's mitt.

A Louisville Slugger baseball bat, Pete Reiser model.

A Captain Easy Big Little Book.

A chrome Gene Autry cap pistol, with red plastic handles.

A sack of marbles, including a couple of "steelies" and a blue cat's-eye taw.

A Captain Marvel decoder ring.

The complete works of Mark Twain.

A genuine leather football helmet, Tom Harmon style.

A Don Budge autographed tennis racquet, with real cat gut strings.

A full set of Tom Swift books.

A hot dog from old Ponce de Leon Park and an Atlanta Crackers' baseball cap shaped like Billy Goodman wore his.

A Buck Rogers ray gun that lights up and makes a "thock-thock-thock" sound.

A Bobby Jones Calamity Jane model putter.

Two Blue Horse tablets and a fountain pen and pencil set.

An original Electric Football Game, not one of those dinky computer things they have now.

Tangerines and jumping beans, licorice twists and a game of Whist, Eskimo Pies and snowy skies, gingerbread with whipped cream spread, peppermints and arrowhead flints, chocolate drops and spinning tops.

Oh, yes. As my one concession to the present, I also need a new copy of Willie Nelson's Christmas album, "Pretty Paper." Mine's all worn out.

197

Thankful for buddies and balloons

November 25, 1982

I'm thankful for...

The pro football strike, because it strengthened my preference for the high school and college game...

Readers who write letters, critical or otherwise...

Writers and announcers who don't treat games like wars...

People you can pay to rake leaves and clean gutters...

Friend Durward Pennington recovering from a heart attack...

Coaches and teachers who teach and care...

Bartenders who laugh and smile a lot...

Willie Nelson albums, Rudyard Kipling stories, Walter Matthau movies and Robert Ludlum books...

Simon and Garfunkle's Concert in the Park on HBO. I've seen it six times...

Dominique Wilkins when it's show time...

Nice, new things like the Izod socks and windbreaker my daughters gave me for my birthday...

Soft, old things like that worn recording of Lena Horne singing "Love Me or Leave Me."...

Good, enjoyable buddies like Stan the biscuit king and Jack the car-wash man...

Buttered grits on a cold morning, oyster stew on a chilly night, and hot dogs with mustard and onions anytime...

Pleasant conversations over cold beers at Henry O's and the Downtowner...

Enjoying the enthusiasm and anticipation of a redheaded, high school cheerleader getting prepared for a Friday night game...

My wife's patience and pancakes...

Golf courses which remain serene even under attack by a spastic game...

Rain, when it's time to go to bed...

Thanksgiving and Christmas, times when people seem to treat each other better...

And having a daughter still young enough to believe in a world of bubblegum, Barbie dolls, bicycles, balloons and rainbows.

Cowboy's last ride

March 22, 1983

They called him Esco (Cowboy) Shaw back when he used to run with a football more than 40 years ago.

His obituary read yesterday that Esco Elliott Shaw was dead at age 59.

I remember Cowboy. I remember as a kid watching him run for the Gainesville High Red Elephants in 1939-40-41. I remember folks said he was college prospect.

But, like so many thousands of his generation Esco saw his football career interrupted by World War II. He and most of his teammates had to go far away to fight with guns rather than play football.

The next time I saw Cowboy was about 1945. He was running with a football again. But this time it was different.

He and some of his teammates, such as Joe Ed Sloan and J. T. Mitchum, were fresh out of the service. Wearing headgears, shoulder pads and sweat suits, they scrimmaged against the GHS team of the day, and helped with some volunteer coaching.

Drane Watson, Gainesville coach at the time, recalls: "Those guys were great help to me as sort of unofficial coaches. They loved football and were just searching for a way to be associated with the game again."

What I remember is Cowboy running the ball again in that scrimmage, despite a slight limp from a war wound suffered as an infantry rifleman in the Italian campaign.

Esco had a brief shot at college ball at Georgia and Clemson, but the years and a war had taken their toll.

I got to know Esco quite well after that and liked him. He loved sports, loved to be around them and loved to talk about them. He laughed and smiled a lot, was a great story teller and enjoyable to be around.

He found all sorts of ways to stay close to athletics. He officiated football, baseball and basketball in these parts for years. He even served as commissioner of Little League baseball here.

I remember once accompanying Esco and his officiating team to a high school football game in a nearby county. The close game ended in controversy and a near riot. As irate fans poured onto the field, Esco and I stood on the sidelines. "What do we do now?" I asked: Esco grinned and said, "We can either stand here and fight or we can run... let's run!" he yelled as we lit out for the parking lot.

We later laughed about the incident over frosty mugs at a country beer joint.

Esco suffered through a number of personal woes in his lifetime. An auto accident took a young son with a bright athletic future. There were long

199

bouts with bad health and some other problems, many of which Esco readily admitted he helped to cause himself.

I hadn't seen Esco much over the past months. But we had talked by phone not too long ago and planned to get together just to shoot the bull again about sports cabbages and kings and other unimportant things.

I don't want to paint Esco as any sort of tragic figure because he really wasn't, not anymore than many of us. But I always viewed him as a man with an unfulfilled dream, but a man I always enjoyed being around.

Yes, I remember Cowboy Shaw. And I liked him. I'm sorry he's gone.

A leather-topped eagle
October 29, 1988

They honored an old friend at Gainesville's Riverside Military Academy the other day.

They named a new barracks for one Col. William D. Maginnis, who for the past 12 progressive years has served as superintendent of that educational institution.

Col. Maginnis is now regarded as a highly successful administrator, and he well deserves every honor they can bestow upon him.

To many longtime Gainesvillians, Maginnis *IS* Riverside Military Academy.

However, if you don't mind, I prefer to remember him as Coach Bill Maginnis who, starting way back in 1951, for many years was head football coach at Riverside.

Bill was one of those old-fashioned, leather helmet coaches because he was at one time himself a leather helmet player.

I remember the many Friday and Saturday afternoons at old Vader Field when Maginnis guided some good Riverside teams, known then as the Blue Battalion.

Most of Maginnis' teams played football as if Knute Rockne had never invented the forward pass. They blocked, tackled, played tough defense and they ran the ball.

You never heard of a Maginnis team ever "getting back to the basics." This is because they never got away from the basics.

Riverside's veteran coach of today, Errol Bisso, played for Maginnis at Riverside, which has a long football tradition that would make another complete story.

I remember Maginnis when he sought out players who had what he called, "the look of the eagle." Bill liked players who had that fiery glint of competitiveness in their eyes. I think it was because Bill himself had it.

It was during the mid- and late-1950's that Maginnis took a brief break from his Riverside career to serve as freshman coach, scout and recruiter for Tulane University, his old school.

In 1955, I accompanied Bill to Atlanta where we witnessed double college football history.

We went to Grant Field to see Georgia Tech play Miami in the first college game ever televised in color. That night, at the same site, we saw Georgia play Ole Miss. It supposedly was the South's first-ever college football doubleheader.

After watching Coach Bobby Dodd's Tech Yellow Jackets beat Miami 14-6 in person and in true living color that afternoon, we adjourned to a nearby Atlanta watering hole where we replayed the Tech game, and Maginnis prepared to scout the Georgia-Ole Miss game for Tulane.

Later, under the lights, Old Miss beat Georgia 26-13 behind a quick and crafty quarterback, and superb punter, named Eagle Day.

As you might know, Maginnis loved that name.

Georgia's quarterback that night is a familiar television figure today. He was Jimmy Harper, now the respected SEC referee with the deep, southern drawl we often hear on televised games.

Oh, by the way. Maginnis also apparently did a solid scouting job that night, because later that season Tulane beat Georgia 14-0.

Maginnis later returned to Riverside where he has been ever since as coach, then principal and now superintendent.

Now my old friend has a barracks named in his honor.

Now he wears a neat uniform when on duty at Riverside.

But I still picture him with a leather helmet on his head.

Because even as a 69-year-old administrator, Bill Maginnis still has "the look of the eagle."

Broadcasting ain't all show biz

November 22, 1988

Just once, I'd like to see one of those big time, big name national play-by-play football announcers try to broadcast a high school game at some sites in North Georgia.

If they did, I guarantee you Pat Summerall would blow his famous cool, Charlie Jones' smoothness would turn to babbling, and they would have to take Brent Musburger away to a padded cell.

The guys on the national level have it easy. They sit in especially designed boxes high in the stadium with a perfect view of the field. Any information they need about any aspect of the game is made available to them. They have the most sophisticated electronic equipment ever devised. It's a snap.

For 31 years I have broadcasted high school football in these parts, and I've done games from some places that would put the national boys into a dead faint.

The last few years of my broadcasting career were not so bad because facilities improved a lot, and I had some fine assistance from broadcast team cohorts like Mike Banks and Robert Parker who made things a lot easier.

But back in the distant past, I started in 1957, you were sometimes lucky just to get on the air, and then get a few clear glimpses of the game.

In Canton that first season, I broadcast a game from the rear bed of a Coca-Cola truck parked above and at the rear of the stands.

When the game ended, the truck driver didn't realize we were still doing the wrapup portion of the broadcast, so he started driving away, ripping out all our wires and sending us sprawling into crates of empty bottles.

We once broadcast from the second floor window of a school building located about 50 yards from the field. In the middle of the third quarter, a janitor who had been nipping a bit heavily on the happy water, came into the room and started cursing us out in loud tones for being there. We had to send for a local cop to get him out.

One year in Danielsville, the only spot available to us was a three-foot high platform on field level near the five-yard line. Once the action moved away from us and passed the 20-yard line, there was no way to tell what was going on.

We used a spotter walking the sidelines to give us pre-arranged hand and arm signals so we could keep up with where the ball was, how many yards were gained and who the runner was.

I've done numerous games from the stands with screaming fans almost in my lap. One year at old Burney-Harris High School in Athens, it rained the entire game and we broadcast under an umbrella held by a guy sitting next to us.

There were plenty of times when there were no yard-line numerals on the field, and you had to do some quick mental mathematics to figure out where the ball was located on every play.

Even the rare times when there were press boxes, they were usually far too small. I've done games with a public address announcer screaming into his mike on my right, an assistant coach yelling into a sideline phone on my left, a movie camera whirring away over the top of my head, and the clock operator, with his control board on his lap, peering out from beneath my elbow.

Each time I hear one of those national broadcasts flowing easily over the air—with no problems about where the ball is, the down, the time left, player identification or anything else—I feel rather smug because the guy doing that game doesn't know what a real challenge is.

Mill league players relive past

April 12, 1989

Lots of people often enjoy a pastime known as "living in the past."

But probably no group gets a bigger kick out of reviving memories than an aging bunch of baseball and basketball players who once competed in the old Industrial Leagues across the Northeast Georgia area.

About 50 of these guys got together once again at the 18th annual Old Timers Reunion held a few nights ago at the Beef Corral on old Atlanta Highway near Gainesville.

Most of them are well past 60 years of age. But they keep showing up to swap old truths, half-truths and just plain lies about those long-past days when they competed against each other purely out of a love for their games.

Some of them now limp on gimpy knees, legs and ankles caused by youthful injuries that now bring on pain revisited by the aging process.

They also recall their teammates and opponents of the past. Unfortunately, the list of the deceased is now getting longer than the number of survivors.

But they keep showing up for talk and laughter, and sometimes even a few tears.

Their names are not legendary on any large scale. But they are among themselves.

Athletes' names were more colorful in those days. Names such as "Blackeye" Kinsey, "Mud" Hudson and "Skyrocket" Smith.

On hand was "Coon" Adams who once played third base for Habersham Mills. "Coon" probably stopped more ground balls with his chest and face than he did with his glove. But he stopped 'em.

I well remember "Birddog" Bailey, a second baseman for Harmony Grove Mills in Commerce. "Birddog" had a grossly deformed left cheek. Mainly due to the presence therein of an estimated nine-pound chaw of tobacco.

There was much talk of the late Dean Evans, player-manager and a fierce competitor for Gainesville Mill.

And Gainesville Mill was one of the places where J. D. "Blossom" Edwards often brandished a talented bat.

203

Tough John Henry Laws, hustling Red Brown and basketball hotshot Paul McDonald were on hand representing Chicopee Mills.

Carrying the colors of New Holland were long and lanky Jake Miller, smiling Bige Hollifield, quiet Eugene Riley, friendly Jim Anglin and entertaining Dub Jones.

Recalling many memories was big Lamar Murphy who was truly a great prospect in the New York Yankees' organization before an arm injury forced him out of the pros and back home to hit brilliantly for Harmony Grove.

Inducted into the group's Blue Ridge Hall of Fame were baseball players Jim Hyder, Ernest Lackey and Aaron Moore, and basketball players Otis McNeal, Alvin Kemp and Jack Jenkins.

Chosen to head up the group and formulate plans for next year's meeting were Buck Cooper, Ernest Lakey and Vic Wilson.

It was truly a wonderful evening for those of us who revel in the pastime of living the past.

Past home runs have gotten longer.

Routine feats have become "great plays."

Old basketball scoring averages have risen dramatically.

All those old .250 hitters now hit "almost .300."

Certainly nothing embellishes like the passage of time, coupled with a competitive imagination.

Taking team loyalty too far

December 4, 1989

We have all heard stories about people who become a bit too emotionally involved in their sports loyalties.

A good example is a couple over in Birmingham, Ala., who are dedicated Auburn football fans.

And they have taken their loyalties out on their children.

Believe it or not, Kay and Larry White have named their children WarEagle and Tiger.

The names are on birth certificates their father carries with him to prove it.

Auburn University's athletic teams are known as Tigers, and their battle cry is "War Eagle."

"My husband and I met on a blind date while we were going to school at Auburn," Mrs. White said. "Needless to say, we're big Auburn fans."

The elder daughter is known as Pepper, but she wishes people would call her WarEagle, her mother said. The youngest daughter has always gone by Tiger.

"The Auburn fans think it's pretty cool," said Pepper WarEagle, an eighth grader.

Aw, come on now, young lady. Auburn fans think orange pickup trucks with big blue wheels are cool.

Tiger, a fourth-grader, is proud of her name. "It's unusual," she said. "No one else has that name. Everyone that hears it says it's cute and unusual."

I'm all for freedom of choice, and I assume parents have a right to name their children anything they so desire.

And I guess this deal is considered a pretty cutesy thing while the children are young, and don't know any better than to think their names are real neat.

But what about when they get a bit older?

More than likely they will want to set fire to wonderful ol' Mom and Dad.

If Kay and Larry White had been Alabama fans I suppose they would have named their daughters Crimson and Tide.

Or maybe Bear and Bryant.

Do Tennessee fans name their daughters Volunteer and Bluetick?

As the father of four daughters, three of them grown, I'm trying to imagine what my girls might already have done to me if I had given them such names.

I went to Gainesville High School so I guess I would have named my oldest daughter Sandy Red Elephant.

Then I went to the University of Georgia, so my second daughter would have been Stacie Bulldog.

I once played on a neighborhood baseball team named the Westside Sluggers, so my third daughter would have been Susan Slugger.

When I was in the Army, I played on a softball team in Korea we named the Dung-chow Dirty Sox.

I'm quire sure my teen-age fourth daughter, Shane Dirty Sox, would have already murdered me multiple times.

When I was on that softball team, we played a medical unit team that called themselves the Pusan Puspockets.

Let us hope none of those medics developed any deep loyalties and passed them on to their children.

If they did, where are you now, Priscilla Puspocket?

The 50-year connection

June 9, 1997

It was both historically and emotionally fitting that the Gainesvill High School Red Elephants baseball team would win its second straight stat championship in the year 1997.

Coach Wayne Vickery's fine baseball team, which set a record in win ning 12 straight playoff games, had both family and traditional connection that go back 50 years.

Two players, pitcher Hutch Evans and pitcher-outfielder Brad Cheste were keys to the connections.

Hutch Evans had a 13-0 mound record and a 1.76 earned run average For his career, he posted a 21-1 record with two no-hitters.

Hutch is the son of Gail and Tommy Evans, an outstanding interio lineman on Gaineville High championship football teams in the 1970's.

Tommy's father was the late Dean Evans, an outstanding local sport figure back in the 1940's.

Dean played pro baseball in the minor leagues, was player-manager o the Gainesville Mill team in the old Georgia-Carolina Industrial League an managed the 1948 industrial league all-star team.

In a brief career as a high school coach, Dean also produced a champion ship basketball team at Gainesville High.

Gainesville's home basefield field is named Ivey-Watson and is locate in the Lanier Point sports complex.

It is named for late coaches Ted Ivey and Drane Watson whose sport careers also go back 50 years.

Watson was coach of all sports at Gainesville High back then, took football team to the state finals in 1947 and coached a baseball team to a stat championship in 1949.

Ivey coached in local youth leagues for years and in 1947 himself wa an athlete, playing for the old McEver Packers and then for Chicopee in th industrial basketball league.

Bradley Chester, Ivey's grandson, completes yet another family connec tion.

Bradley's father, David Chester, was himself an outstanding Gainesvill High pitcher in the 1960's.

Colleene Ivey, Ted's wife, David's mother and Bradley's grandmother provided personal and spectator support during the sports careers.

And there was another bit of tradition on hand in the person of on George Groover, Gainesville High's legendary supporter and unofficial man ager of all Red Elephant athletic teams over the past 50 years.

It was about 1947 when Groover, just a young boy, first started hanging around the practice sessions and games of Gainesville High teams.

Groover and his loyalty have been right on the scene ever since.

Certainly these are not the only 50-year connections to exist in this area. And certainly they all have one thing in common.

There have always been far more cheers than jeers.